HARRIS COUNTY PUBLIC LIBRARY

• 3 4028 05599 2482

973.045 Ita
The Italians

APR 0 4 2005

$34.95
ocm56334165

⌀ W9-BYJ-427

COMING TO AMERICA

THE ITALIANS

C.J. Shane, *Book Editor*

Bruce Glassman, *Vice President*
Bonnie Szumski, *Publisher*
Helen Cothran, *Managing Editor*

GREENHAVEN PRESS
An imprint of Thomson Gale, a part of The Thomson Corporation

THOMSON
————— ✶ —————
GALE

Detroit • New York • San Francisco • San Diego • New Haven, Conn.
Waterville, Maine • London • Munich

THOMSON

★

GALE ™

© 2005 Thomson Gale, a part of The Thomson Corporation.

Thomson and Star Logo are trademarks and Gale and Greenhaven Press are registered trademarks used herein under license.

For more information, contact
Greenhaven Press
27500 Drake Rd.
Farmington Hills, MI 48331-3535
Or you can visit our Internet site at http://www.gale.com

ALL RIGHTS RESERVED.
No part of this work covered by the copyright hereon may be reproduced or used in any form or by any means—graphic, electronic, or mechanical, including photocopying, recording, taping, Web distribution or information storage retrieval systems—without the written permission of the publisher.

Every effort has been made to trace the owners of copyrighted material.

Cover credit: © AP/Wide World Photos. A member of the Bronx's Pelham Panthers bocce team makes a shot during a city-wide tournament in New York's Little Italy in 1996.

Library of Congress, 38, 109, 116, 191

LIBRARY OF CONGRESS CATALOGING-IN-PUBLICATION DATA

The Italians / C.J. Shane, book editor.
   p. cm. — (Coming to America)
Includes bibliographical references and index.
ISBN 0-7377-2765-9 (lib. : alk. paper)
   1. Italian Americans—History. 2. Immigrants—United States—History. 3. Italian Americans—Social conditions. 4. Italian Americans—Biography. I. Shane, C.J.
II. Coming to America (San Diego, Calif.)
E184.I8I837 2005
973'.0451'00922—dc22   2004054132

Printed in the United States of America

CONTENTS

the state of Oklahoma) assimilated more slowly than elsewhere in the United States. The immigrant women maintained Italian traditions in courtship, marriage, and family life.

Chapter 2: The Italians' New Life in America

who had grown up in America. Although many ethnic groups were involved in organized crime, it was Italian Americans who became stereotyped as criminals.

Chapter 3: From Immigration to Assimilation

Chapter 4: Profiles of Famous Italian Americans

FOREWORD

In her popular novels, such as *The Joy Luck Club* and *The Bonesetter's Daughter*, Chinese American author Amy Tan explores the complicated cultural and social differences between Chinese-born mothers and their American-born daughters. For example, the mothers eat foods and hold religious beliefs that their daughters either abhor or abstain from, while the daughters pursue educational and career opportunities that were not available to the previous generation. Generation gaps occur in almost all families, but as Tan's writings show, such differences are even more pronounced when parents grow up in a different country. When immigrants come to the United States, their initial goal is often to start a new life that is an improvement from the life they experienced in their homeland. However, while these newcomers may intend to fully adapt to American culture, they inevitably bring native customs with them. Immigrants have helped make America broader culturally by introducing new religions, languages, foods, and different ways of looking at the world. Their children and subsequent generations, however, often seek to cast aside these traditions and instead more fully absorb mainstream American mores.

As Tan's writings suggest, the dissimilarities between immigrants and their children are manifested in several ways. Adults who come to the United States and do not learn English turn to their children, educated in the American school system, to serve as interpreters and translators. Children, seeing what their American-born schoolmates eat, reject the foods of their native land. Religion is another area where the generation gap is particularly pronounced. For example, the liturgy of Syrian Christian services had to be translated into English when most young Syrian Americans no longer knew how to speak Syriac. Numerous Jews, freed from the European ghettos they had lived in, wished to assimilate more fully into the surrounding culture and began to loosen the traditional dietary and ritual requirements under which they had grown up. Reformed Judaism, which began in Germany, thus found a strong foothold among young Jews born in America.

However, no generational experiences have been as significant as that between immigrant mothers and their daughters. Living in the United States has afforded girls and young women opportunities they likely would not have had in their homelands. The daughters of immigrants, in some cases, live entirely different lives than their mothers did in their native nations. Where an Arab mother may have only received a limited education, her American-raised daughter enjoys a full course of American public schooling, often continuing on to college and careers. A woman raised in India might have been placed in an arranged marriage, while her daughter will have the opportunity to date and choose a husband. Admittedly, not all families have been willing to give their daughters all these new freedoms, but these American-born girls are frequently more willing to declare their wishes.

The generation gap is only one aspect of the immigrant experience in the United States. Understanding immigrants' unique and shared experiences and their contributions to American life is an interesting way to study the many people who make up the American citizenry. Greenhaven Press's Coming to America series helps readers learn why more people have moved to the United States than to any other nation. Selections on the lives of immi-

grants once they have reached America, from their struggles to find employment to their experiences with discrimination and prejudice, help give students insights into
stereotypes and cultural mores that continue to this day.
Finally, profiles of prominent immigrants help the reader
become aware of the many achievements of these people
in fields ranging from science to politics to sports.

Each volume in the Coming to America series takes an
extensive look into a particular immigrant population. The
carefully selected primary and secondary sources provide
both historical perspectives and firsthand insights into the
immigrant experience. Combined with an in-depth introduction and a comprehensive chronology and bibliogra-
phy, every book in the series is a valuable addition to the
study of American history. With immigrants comprising
nearly 12 percent of the U.S. population, and their children and grandchildren constantly adding to the population, the immigrant experience continues to evolve. Coming to America is consequently a beneficial tool for not
only understanding America's past but also its future.

INTRODUCTION

In the late nineteenth century, thousands of Italian peasants fled the poverty of their homeland to seek a better life in America. Most came from the southern regions of Italy, especially the island of Sicily, where they had been working as agricultural laborers on the estates of wealthy landowners. Most were also poverty-stricken and uneducated, and had few prospects when they arrived in America. However, like other immigrant groups who made vital contributions to American life, Italian immigrants worked and saved, educated their children, struggled against prejudice, and persevered until they achieved the American dream. Many succeeded and made significant contributions to every aspect of American life, including business, politics, sports, and the arts. By the 1960s, Italian Americans were so well integrated into American society that many bemoaned their complete assimilation and loss of ethnic Italian culture.

Despite these achievements and successes, Italian Americans have been plagued with a unique problem that other immigrant groups have escaped. From the 1880s to the present, Italian Americans have been consistently labeled as a people involved in crime. A second stereotype of Italians as boorish and crude also emerged in the early twentieth century, and to no surprise, this caricature also often included an association with gangsters. Stereotyping of Italian Americans as mobsters is so pervasive that most Americans seem unaware of how casually the stereotype is accepted and how it sometimes frustrates Italian Americans.

Italian Immigration and American Nativism

Italians who immigrated to the United States before 1880 came primarily from the more economically developed northern regions of Italy. Many of these early immigrants, who arrived in relatively small numbers before 1880, were educated and often had special skills, especially in the artisan trades such as stone cutting and building. The artisans were in demand in a young America busily constructing itself from the ground up. These Italian immigrants were accepted into American society because of their skills, and also because they were seen as the inheritors of a glorious culture that includes ancient Roman civilization and the Italian Renaissance.

This generally positive view of Italians changed dramatically after 1880 when a flood of immigrants from the poorest regions of southern Italy began to arrive on American shores. By World War II, nearly one-fourth of Italy's entire population had emigrated. Most came to the United States, although some went to other destinations, especially Argentina. The majority of the immigrants who came to the United States were pushed by poverty and prejudice into crowded slums in eastern cities, where they worked primarily as laborers in industries such as construction, mining, and New England's textile trade.

The United States was experiencing episodic economic recessions in the 1880s and 1890s, and many Americans were concerned about job security. A type of thinking especially hostile to immigrants known as nativism took hold in many American minds. Nativists argued that America and American ways should be protected from immigrants who did not come from the preferred northern European countries such as England, Scandinavia, and Germany. The immigrants from southern Europe, Asia, and Latin America could not be assimilated into American society, the nativists claimed, and furthermore, the immigrants stole jobs from American-born workers.

Italian Americans were only one of several immigrant groups directly affected by nativist claims. The Chinese were denied the right to immigrate in 1882 under the Chinese Exclusion Act, and in the American Southwest, landownership and civil rights were gradually stripped from Mexican Americans. Nativists claimed that the Chinese, the Mexicans, and the Italians were all morally and culturally deficient and incapable of assimilation. Calls for restriction on their immigration became more common. Scholar Donald Tricarico explains the attitude of the time toward Italian immigrants: "At its core was the view that Italians were not only different from, but inferior to, the Anglo-Saxon race stock of the American majority."[1]

As well as being considered inferior, Italian immigrants were feared because they were labeled as criminals. Many

Americans had read news reports of Italian criminal organizations and began to believe that most Italians entering the United States were members of one particular criminal gang in Italy known as the Mafia. It was widely believed that the Italian immigrants continued their Mafia criminal activities in America. In reality, Americans understood little about the true nature of the Mafia and were wrong in concluding that all Italian immigrants were criminals.

In the nineteenth century, Italy was fragmented into small states and had been repeatedly overrun by foreign powers. In response to the resulting political and economic chaos, local groups emerged in an effort to create stability. The Mafia, based entirely in a small region of western Sicily, was one such group. Most members had family ties. The Mafia relied on personal influence, frequently made deals with corrupt local officials, and sometimes engaged in violent and other criminal activities in order to ensure the welfare of its members and influence the outcome of events. Other organizations similar to the Mafia, such as the Naples-based Camorra, also existed in southern Italy, but somehow only the Mafia became well known to Americans. Despite claims to the contrary by American nativists, the Mafia was too dependent on local connections to be transferred to any other country. Although individual Mafia members immigrated to the United States, the Sicilian Mafia as an organization never became a significant factor in American criminal society.

A small percentage of Italian immigrants were involved in crime in nineteenth-century America. Most of the criminals were young, disaffected immigrant men with few prospects. A few were former Mafiosi who had immigrated to America. These petty criminals in America's urban slums formed a loose-knit association of gangs called the Black Hand in the late nineteenth century. Black Hand gang members preferred to prey off their fellow Italian immigrants by using the threat of violence to extort money rather than go to work as laborers.

The Sicilian Mafia continued to engage the imagination of the American public, however, and Black Hand gang members were assumed to be Mafiosi. In the 1890s, violent or criminal acts involving Italians were routinely attributed to the Mafia. Many Americans began to assume that all Italian immigrants were members of the Mafia, all Mafia members were criminals, and therefore all Italian immigrants were criminals. Even late into the twentieth century, the word *Mafia* would be used inaccurately, sometimes even by law enforcement officials, to describe the activities of what were actually American organized crime groups that included ethnic Italian members.

The early stereotyping of Italians as criminal Mafiosi led to tragic results in New Orleans. In 1890 the city's chief of police was murdered, and eleven Italian immigrant merchants were accused of being Mafia members and of killing the police chief. All eleven were arrested. In the ensuing court case, the Italians were either found innocent or their charges were dismissed for lack of evidence.

Unsatisfied with the court decision, a mob led by a white supremacist lynched the Italians in 1891. Especially galling to the lynch mob was the fact that the Italian merchants had allowed blacks to purchase items at Italian-owned stores and had even called the black customers "Mister." The lynching was understandable, according to several newspapers and citizens groups of the time, because of the assumed link between Italians and the criminal Mafia. The *New York Times* wrote:

> These sneaking and cowardly Sicilians, the descendants of bandits and assassins, who have transported to this country the lawless passions, the cut-throat practices, the oath-bound societies of their native country, are to us a pest without mitigation.[2]

There is no evidence, however, that the Italian merchants were members of any criminal organization. In addition to the lynchings in New Orleans, there were many more incidents of Italian immigrants being harassed, beat up, and unfairly accused of crimes by native-born Americans in the late nineteenth and early twentieth centuries.

The Red Scare, Prohibition, and World War II

The Italian immigrant as Mafia member was just one stereotype Americans held about Italian immigrants. Another was that of the Italian immigrants as political radicals who were in turn linked to crime. Many Americans began to fear that the Italian immigrant radicals would try to bring down the American government or damage American business. Although it is true that many Italian Americans were part of the emerging labor movement in the early twentieth century, it is inaccurate to say that all Italian immigrants and labor union organizers were radicals who used violence as a tactic.

America was rapidly industrializing in the late nineteenth and early twentieth centuries, and many businessmen and industrialists (often called "robber barons") made their fortunes in this era of unregulated capitalism. Italian immigrants and immigrants from many other nations provided the labor in the mines and factories owned by the new industrialists. Unions and labor rights were virtually nonexistent, and working conditions were often horrendous. In the textile factories of New England, for example, workers started in the textile mills at the age of fourteen, and over one-third of them died before the age of twenty-five because of accidents and unhealthy work conditions. In 1911, 145 immigrant women workers perished in the fire at the Triangle Shirtwaist Factory in New York City because the factory owners had locked the workers inside the building. The young immigrant workers could not escape the flames. More than half of the dead were Italian immigrants.

When a labor rights movement emerged in the early 1900s, Italian immigrants were active in the formation of unions and in the organization of strikes for better wages and better working conditions. Many of the early immigrant labor organizers were either socialists or anarchists. Both socialism and anarchism had great influence in Europe at this time, but these political philosophies were deeply distrusted in the United States.

By 1917 the Russian Revolution was held up to Americans as an example of the social and economic chaos that could result from radical political and economic philosophies. Concern about radicalism was so great that America entered a period known as the Red Scare. Pervasive suspicion was directed toward leaders of the American labor movement, many of whom were Italians. Therefore, in addition to being stereotyped as common criminals, the Italians were also branded as violent radicals involved in illegal and criminal activity. The vast majority of Italian immigrants disavowed violence and crime, but they could not overcome the criminal stereotype now associated with labor organizing. This criminal stereotype connected to political radicalism came to a head in the case of Sacco and Vanzetti.

Nicola Sacco and Bartolomeo Vanzetti, both Italian immigrants, were arrested, tried, and ultimately executed for murders that occurred during a bank robbery in 1920. Anti-Italian prejudice prevailed throughout their trial. To this day, historians do not know whether Sacco and Vanzetti were guilty of the crime, but they agree that the two did not receive a fair trial, largely because they were both Italians and political radicals. The two became victims of Italian immigrant stereotypes and the Red Scare. Although some Americans may have breathed a sigh of relief when Sacco and Vanzetti were executed in 1927, they may not have realized that a much larger problem was brewing—the development of organized crime.

During the Prohibition era of the 1920s and 1930s, organized crime emerged on a large scale in the United States. The production and sale of alcoholic beverages were prohibited by law during Prohibition. Seeing an economic opportunity, American criminals entered the illegal beverage trade in large numbers. The majority of Prohibition-era criminals were American-born, not immigrants, and some of these criminals were Italian American. The most famous was Al Capone, the son of an Italian immigrant, who headed a multiethnic criminal organization composed of Italians, Slavs, Jews, Irish, and other ethnic groups. Americans were fascinated with Capone, and his Italian ethnicity contributed to the persistent view that all Italian Americans were criminals.

The start of World War II further set back the cause of Italian acceptance into American society because one of America's enemies in the war was Italy. Suspicion against Italian immigrants and Italian Americans was strong enough during the war that many Italian American families were forced by U.S. government officials to relocate from the California coast for fear that they might assist Italian enemy infiltrators. Some Italian Americans were even put into internment camps for the duration of the war. During this time, Italian Americans experienced both subtle and blatant forms of prejudice, including having to endure insults about their Italian ethnicity.

The Language of Prejudice

Most immigrant groups have been tagged with terms meant to insult and degrade their members. In the case of Italians, the most common insults, beginning in the 1880s, were "wop," "dago," and "guinea." *Wop* means "without papers" and refers to Italians who may have immigrated illegally. *Dago* may be a mispronunciation of "Diego," a common Spanish name, suggesting that many Americans had difficulty differentiating Spanish and Italian immigrants. *Guinea* likely came from the name of a country in West Africa where many African slaves originated and probably refers to the dark skin of the southern Italian immigrants.

In the 1970s, "guido" became a popular derogatory term for Italian Americans. Guido is actually a favorite first name in Italian families, but it began to be used by some Americans to insult Italian Americans. According to scholar Pellegrino D'Acierno, *guido* is "a pejorative term applied to lower-class, macho, gold-amulet-wearing, self-displaying neighborhood boys." This image, he says, has been the "dominant mass-media stereotype projected onto Italian American young men since the 1970s." A "guidette" is a guido's "gum-chewing, big-haired, air-headed female counterpart."[3]

The guido image was part of a second stereotype of Italian Americans that developed in tandem with the image of the Italian American criminal. According to this stereotype, the Italian male was crude and boorish, barely literate, and hardly able to string together a coherent sentence. The female Italian American was seen as passive, stupid, and fat.

Examples of the language of prejudice—words such as *wop*, *dago*, and *guinea*—are not often heard in contemporary America. However, the term *guido* appears regularly in the media and popular culture. Accompanying these terms are images that are no less prejudiced.

Popular Culture Before World War II

Prejudicial images of Italian Americans have been part of American popular culture since the days of the great Italian immigration. Newspaper cartoons regularly depicted Italian immigrants as degenerates or buffoons in the nineteenth and early twentieth centuries. When films first appeared in the 1920s, Italian immigrants often found themselves portrayed as gangsters. For example, Edward G. Robinson starred as an Italian American gangster in *Little Caesar* (1930) and in *Scarface* (1932).

When these films were being released, few Italian Americans had influential positions in the film industry. One rare exception was the director Frank Capra. He never made films explicitly about Italian Americans, but many film historians believe that Capra's films, such as *It's a Wonderful Life*, exemplify the values that he learned from his Italian immigrant parents—home, family, hard work, kindness toward others, and support for the community. These values stand in sharp contrast with the way most Italian Americans were portrayed in the films of the day.

During this period before television, Americans relied on newspaper cartoons, comic books, and radio programs for entertainment. Again, in comics and on the radio, Italian Americans were painted with a broad brush as criminals, as ignorant boors, or as both boorish and criminal. For example, the cartoon character Dick Tracy, created by Chester Gould, struggled against his enemy Big Boy, a character drawn to look like Al Capone. Many of Tracy's cartoon enemies had Italian-sounding names, such as Ben Spaldoni, Ribs Mocco, and Danny Supeena. "Gould's representation of Italian Americans as incorrigible gangsters remained the approved caricature of Italian Americans in comic books for years,"[4] according to historians Luciano J. Iorizzo and Salvatore Mondello. Other superheroes, including Batman and Captain Marvel, also fought Italian American gangsters.

Ethnic stereotyping was common in comedy routines as well. In the 1920s and 1930s the Marx brothers—Chico, Harpo, Groucho, Zeppo, and Gummo—all took Italian-sounding names and performed vaudeville comedy routines (and later films) that mimicked and poked fun at Italians. "The success of the Marx brothers is based in part upon a crude caricature of the early Italian immigrants in the United States,"[5] claim Iorizzo and Mondello.

World War II caused a shift in American popular culture. Whereas before the comic book villains had all been Italian mobsters, once the war began German Nazis and Japanese kamikaze pilots became the demons to be vilified or lampooned in comics, on the radio, and in Hollywood films. Italian American criminals became less prominent in popular culture—at least until after the war.

Popular Culture After World War II

Not long after World War II was over, American pop culture left behind the Nazi and Japanese villains to focus again on Italian American gangsters as the bad guys. In 1948 actor Edward G. Robinson reappeared in his favorite guise as an Italian mobster as Johnny Rocco in the film *Key Largo*. In the comics, heroes returned to fighting criminals with Italian names. Television became common in many American homes in the mid-1950s, and it provided yet another medium to convey the stereotype of Italian American criminals. The Italian American gangster was prominently featured in a popular series set in the Prohibition era called *The Untouchables*, which began broadcasting in 1959. In the same year, Rod Steiger played Al Capone in a Hollywood film by the same name.

Any hope of separating Italian Americans from the criminal stereotype was undermined in 1972 with the debut of what is often called the greatest gangster film of all time, *The Godfather*, directed by Francis Ford Coppola and based on the novel by Mario Puzo. In the novel, Puzo directly links the Sicilian Mafia to Italian American organized crime. Coppola's film had tremendous impact on the public because it was such a compelling story and its images of Italian American life and culture were so rich and vivid. Puzo's novel and Coppola's film portrayal of the Mafia leader Corleone were different from earlier Italian gangster portrayals because, for the first time, a gangster was depicted as a loving father and family man who faithfully followed his own system of honor. Coppola went on to make two more *Godfather* films, and his work initiated a frenzy of interest in the Mafia and gangsters in American popular culture. However, some Italian Americans see Coppola's films as a disaster for all Italian Americans because the films permanently etched in most Americans' minds the stereotype of Italian Americans as criminals.

Other films took up the "guido" theme in the 1970s and after. The classic guido is Tony Manero, played by John Travolta, in the 1977 film *Saturday Night Fever*. Tony has a going-nowhere job in a paint store and lives only to disco dance on Saturday nights. He eventually escapes his dead-end life, but the cost is leaving behind his Italian ethnicity, portrayed as boorish and ignorant. Rocky Balboa in *Rocky* (1976) is the ultimate inarticulate boor who moves up from being a small-time bouncer and tough guy to become a successful prizefighter. *Married to the Mob* (1988) and *My Cousin Vinny* (1992) are two more examples of "guido" films. It was not long before guido developed a criminal component to his personality. The Italian American mobster in the 1985 movie *Prizzi's Honor* is both boorish and a dangerous hit man.

A Stereotype Lives On

The popular HBO television series *The Sopranos* is a contemporary example of the continuing portrayal in American popular culture of Italian Americans involved in criminal activity. The series is about an Italian American family headed by Tony Soprano, a Mafia-linked mobster under the care of a psychiatrist for anxiety attacks. Mundane family matters are intertwined with scenes of violence associated with gangster criminal activities. Journalist Joe Cappo criticizes the ethnic stereotyping in *The Sopranos*, which he calls a "Mafia fairy tale." Cappo, who says his Italian immigrant grandfathers and father worked on the railroad and in the post office and were never Mafia hit men, appeals to the media moguls to portray Italian Americans more accurately:

> I have grown tired of this constant depiction of Italian-Americans as mobsters and only as mobsters. I am offended by the reaction of many members of the media who tell us to "get over it.". . . People all over the world associate all Italians with the Mafia. . . . It's time you goodfellas paid back. Before you make yet another mob movie, why don't you produce a work in which Italian-Americans are involved in something other than crime— like music, business, art, sports, science, politics, literature . . . even movies? In other words, do something different for a change.[6]

The National Italian American Foundation (NIAF) makes a point of informing the public and media of persistent Italian American stereotyping. For example, in the spring of 2004, NIAF expressed concern about ethnic stereotyping in a new animated film from DreamWorks titled *Shark Tale*. According to NIAF, "The DreamWorks website describes *Shark Tale* as a 'gangster comedy' that features sharks as mafia characters with Italian names that belong to the 'Five Families.'"[7] Filmmaker Spike Lee's latest film *She Hate Me* (2004) also has been criticized by film critic Richard Roeper for ethnic stereotyping of Italian Americans.

Thus, the stereotype of Italian Americans as gangsters with connections to the Mafia persists into the twenty-first century even though it would be far more accurate to describe Italian Americans as contributors to society rather than as criminals. In the following collection of essays, scholars reveal many aspects of Italian immigrant life: the poverty the immigrants escaped in nineteenth-century Italy; their hard work to build a new life in America in places like New York, California, and Oklahoma; their gradual assimilation into American society; and the many contributions they have made on behalf of the United States. Yet throughout this history of achievement and success, there is a thread of persistent stereotyping that unfairly connects Italian Americans with a life of crime.

Notes

1. Donald Tricarico, "Labels and Stereotypes," in Salvatore J. LaGumina et al., eds., *The Italian-American Experience: An Encyclopedia.* New York: Garland, 2000, p. 319.

2. Quoted in Luciano J. Iorizzo and Salvatore Mondello, *The Italian Americans.* Boston: Twayne, 1980, p. 85.

3. Pellegrino D'Acierno, "Cultural Lexicon," in Pellegrino D'Acierno, ed., *The Italian American Heritage: A Companion to Literature and Arts.* New York: Garland, 1999, p. 730.

4. Iorizzo and Mondello, *The Italian Americans*, p. 271.

5. Iorizzo and Mondello, *The Italian Americans*, p. 267.

6. Joe Cappo, "Time to Rub Out Tired Mafia-Themed Movies," *Crain's Chicago Business*, June 19, 2001, p. 8.

7. National Italian American Foundation, "Picks and Pans," Spring 2004. www.niaf.org/image_identity/ppSpring2004.asp.

CHAPTER 1

The Great Wave of Immigration

COMING TO AMERICA

Why the Italians Left Italy

Andrew F. Rolle

Although Italians immigrated to America throughout the nineteenth century, the immigration rate soared between 1880 and 1910. Over 5 million Italians, most from the southern regions of the country, left their homeland, boarding ships for New York City and other port cities in the United States. There were many reasons for the massive emigration from Italy, according to historian Andrew F. Rolle. Periodic famines and extreme poverty were foremost among them. Agricultural lands in southern Italy were eroded and barren. The tax system favored the wealthy, who owned most of the land. Even in the best of times, Italian laborers and peasants often went hungry. The political situation also was a factor. Before Italy was finally unified in the 1870s, it had been repeatedly invaded by foreign troops, making life even harder. In the face of all these struggles, going to America was not only a romantic and adventurous idea; it also was a rational choice for poverty-stricken peasants hoping to improve their lives. In this selection, Rolle, a professor of history at Occidental College in Los Angeles, describes these conditions influencing Italians' decision to leave their country. Rolle is the author of *The Immigrant Upraised: Italian Adventures and Colonists in an Expanding America* and *Italian Americans: Troubled Roots.*

Before the *Risorgimento*[1] brought Italy a tardy unification [in the nineteenth century], she was plagued by foreign

1. the "Resurrection" movement for unification and independence

Andrew F. Rolle, *The Immigrant Upraised: Italian Adventurers and Colonists in an Expanding America.* Norman: University of Oklahoma Press, 1968. Copyright © 1968 by the University of Oklahoma Press. Reproduced by permission.

armies tramping over her countryside. Throughout much of the nineteenth century, Italy was at the mercy of a reactionary Austria or an invading France. Such foreign interventions were bound to provoke an eventual exodus. Political repression created prominent exiles, among them the political philosopher Filippo Mazzei, as well as Mozart's librettist Lorenzo Da Ponte, and the patriot Giuseppe Garibaldi, who for a time sought asylum in the United States. Most Italians, however, moved to the New World for reasons other than political. The whole tide of events seemed to flow against them at home. The gap between Italy's expectations and reality discouraged individual enterprise.

Social, economic, and political conditions usually best explain why immigrants left their native land in search of new homes. From the eighteenth to the twentieth centuries, conditions on the Italian peninsula encouraged the departure of hundreds of thousands of persons for the farthest reaches of the Western Hemisphere. A glance at the Italy of past epochs helps one to understand not only why immigrants left but also the role of this nationality in the New World.

Hunger for Food and for Land

Periodic famines were almost endemic, even in Italy's breadbasket provinces. Furthermore, unprecedented taxation (at one time twenty-two different taxes were levied upon landholdings) and widespread unemployment caused perennial discontent. Land was hopelessly restricted to monopolistic owners, and in overpopulated provinces the soil belonged to the nobility; tenants were frequently leaseholders or landless agricultural workers who labored for a pittance. Landlords demanded high rent and a sizable proportion of peasant crops, leaving little for these laborers to live on in the winter months. The phrase *"chi ha prato ha tutto"* (whoever has land has everything) summed-up the fact that by the nineteenth century a dynastic land elite monopolized Italy's future.

In contrast to this unattainable land stood the sparsely settled, unclaimed, distant American West. The vastness of America, a vision of hope, extended inland from her eastern shores for three thousand miles. Whereas in the Old World land was scarce and men were many, in the New World there was much land and few men. . . .

For centuries Italy's peasants struggled with a parched, stubborn, and eroded soil. Poor rainfall, lessened by the many high mountain barriers, further reduced the tillable acreage. Small peasant villages, their topsoil drained away by centuries of erosion, dotted the land—cliff-hanging, barren, rocky remnants. Elsewhere, scorched and sandy plots of terrain, perennially lacking in water, made the growing of crops at best marginal. In the south, rain was either unpredictably scarce or so abundant as to cause floods. In the nineteenth century, peasants living in its swamps and marshes were at the mercy of cholera, which ravaged the villages of Italy.

Except for Portugal, no country in Europe had a lower consumption of meat per inhabitant. In some of Italy's southern provinces the peasant diet consisted of little more than bread and water, with macaroni available a few times a week and meat only once in a while. Statistics dramatize the difference between the standards of life in Europe and in America. In 1880, the average Italian each year consumed only 28 pounds of meat, at a time when the United States led the world with a consumption of 120 pounds per capita. Italy had a deficit of 5,000,000 bushels of wheat that year while the United States enjoyed a surplus of 150,000,000 bushels. The Italians, traditionally great eaters of *pasta* products, had every incentive to look enviously toward the United States, and particularly toward the agricultural areas of the American West, where their most desired foods—grain and meat—were to be found in abundance.

Little Hope for Peasants

For prospective immigrants, the alternative to this affluence was to stay on in a country where life not only was increasingly debased but social apathy prevented the correction of inequality. How the poorest sections of Italy felt about their plight was obvious after 1870. Only with difficulty could uprisings of starving *contadini* [peasant farmers] be suppressed by the governments which followed the union of Italy that year. Throughout the 1880's bread riots broke out in many cities as well as in the rural districts of Lombardy, Calabria, and Sicily. In these provinces peasants living below a subsistence level joined the indignant unemployed of the cities in violent revolt. During that decade these demonstrations, however, ended in frustrating governmental repressions, as did later outbreaks in Milan against grain shortages and a tax on flour milling.

The disparity between relative wealth in Italy's north and abject poverty in the south remained unmistakable. Carlo Levi, in his book *Christ Stopped at Eboli*, poignantly describes the wretched living conditions among the peasants of Lucania in southern Italy:

> The peasants' houses were all alike, consisting of only one room that served as kitchen, bedroom, and usually as quarters for the barnyard animals as well, unless there happened to be an outhouse. . . . On one side of the room was the stove; sticks brought in every day from the fields served as fuel, and the walls and ceiling were blackened with smoke. The only light was that from the door. The room was almost entirely filled by an enormous bed, much larger than an ordinary double bed; in it slept the whole family, father, mother, and children. The smallest children, before they were weaned, that is until they were three or four years old, were kept in little reed cradles or

baskets hung from the ceiling just above the bed. When the mother wanted to nurse them she did not have to get out of bed; she simply reached out and pulled the baby down to her breast, then put him back and with one motion of her hand made the basket rock like a pendulum until he had ceased to cry.

Under the bed slept the animals, and so the room was divided into three layers: animals on the floor, people in the bed, and infants in the air. When I bent over a bed to listen to a patient's heart or to give an injection to a woman whose teeth were chattering with fever or who was burning up with malaria, my head touched the hanging cradles, while frightened pigs and chickens darted between my legs.

Concerning the peasants' feelings about America, Levi writes:

The Kingdom of Naples has perished, and the kingdom of the hopelessly poor is not of this world. Their other world is America. Even America, to the peasants, has a dual nature. It is a land where a man goes to work, where he toils and sweats for his daily bread, where he lays aside a little money only at the cost of endless hardship and privation, where he can die and no one will remember him. At the same time, and with no contradiction in terms, it is an earthly paradise and the promised land.

Another Italian writer, Danilo Dolci, has also described the discouragingly hopeless attitude of Sicily's peasants. If he today finds an inexorable fatalism in them, one can well imagine their instinctive distrust of "progress" on the Italian peninsula. Not even neighbors could be trusted in such a society. The government was always regarded as by its nature an enemy. There was no idea of co-operative enterprise, no belief in the possibility of agricultural improvement or indeed of any progress at all. One prerequisite of social reform is the capacity to look forward, and in Sicily the lack of this ability undoubtedly presented the biggest obstacle of all—the dialect did not even possess a future tense.

No Political Role for Common People

Furthermore, most of the Italian people during the late nineteenth century had no feeling of involvement in the process of unification, Indeed, in Italy's provinces the rural multitudes, wedded to parochial loyalties, were often against national unity. All too often the aristocracy did not comprehend the peasantry. Frequently the politicians did not understand the city masses. And monarchs did but little to alleviate the misery of the people. At a time when the national focus should have been directed toward internal improvements, Italy's lethargic and inefficient bureaucracy concerned itself with colonial aspirations beyond the ken of the Italian people—only to be thwarted in various attempts to build up overseas colonies in North Africa and in the Mediterranean.

After 1878, partly as a result of the Congress of Berlin, Italy began to feel self-conscious about her lack of colonies. With the English guarding Gibraltar and Suez, the Mediterranean aspirations of Italian politicos came alive. In Eritrea and Abyssinia, Italy saw a last chance to carve out an African "sphere of interest," as the large powers now labeled their colonialism. In 1887, Italy sent a poorly prepared army into Abyssinia.

But, following fifteen years of almost constant fighting. Italy was able to retain only narrow strips of land (Eritrea and Somalia) along the coast of the Red Sea. In 1912, after a war with Turkey, the Italians took Tripoli on the south shore of the Mediterranean. The cost of these military adventures, however, reduced Italy almost to bankruptcy. Never a rich country, she increased taxation to support armaments expenditures. Since these taxes fell largely on the poor, hundreds of thousands of Italians were further encouraged to leave their homeland.

The power struggle between pope and king also had discouraging effects. For decades the country was hampered by this unsatisfactory church-state relationship. Critics of the church summarized their feelings by the phrase *"Siamo sotto le unghi dei preti."* (We are under the talons of the priests.) Oppressed thus by the church and by burdensome taxation for the maintenance of a growing army and navy, Italy's poor suffered. Usurious rates of interest on loans rose as high as 50 per cent.

National Economic Problems

Italy's inability to mechanize, added to her feeble economic growth, industrial lag, and unimaginative leadership, intensified the appeal of the outside world to her workers. In the overcrowded cities, delayed industrialization and uneven economic advance was the rule. Healthy economic growth does not flourish in times of political disorder and floundering national purpose. A hostile social climate augurs, instead, meager opportunity and few jobs. Such events as the cholera epidemic of 1887—plus an apathetic national mentality, monarchical problems, constitutional crises, and misunderstanding between classes—created widespread public frustration.

In addition, Italy suffered from ineradicable physical handicaps, among them earthquakes, droughts, floods, malaria, and depleted soil and mineral resources (especially coal and iron). As the population after the turn of the century reached a density of 113 persons per square mile, vast tracts of land, located sometimes in pestiferous swamps and inaccessible mountain ranges, remained uninhabitable.

Depressed by a psychology of scarcity, little wonder that whole villages became depopulated, or *spopolati*, as provincials grew accustomed to a migrant life. During 1900 an estimated million workers spent up to two months annually working away from their families in other provinces. In time whole towns were literally split in two, half their population in Italy, the rest on the other side of the ocean. In 1901 the mayor of the South Italian town of Moliterno, introducing Italy's visiting prime minister, said: "I greet you in the name of eight thousand fellow citizens, three thousand of whom are in America, and the other five thousand preparing to follow them.". . .

The Role of Adventure

One should not overlook the role of adventure in the decision to go to the New World. Indefinite attitudes based on feeling and mood especially influenced romantic young adventurers who headed for the American West. More tangible factors relating to the young, however, included their desire to escape military conscription, parental domination, and rural immobility. Far from restraints and traditions of all sorts the West represented the least controlled of environments. Its flamboyance and very adolescence appealed to youthful spirits. So did the incredible "Westward Movement." This frontier challenge of "the known meeting the unknown" produced a particular fascination. Louis Adamic, a Yugoslav, described how the writing of James Fenimore Cooper, with its legendry of Indians and cowboys, acted as a magnet: "my chief motive in emigrating was not the hope of economic betterment, but a desire for excitement and adventure."

The search for the primeval, a recurrent theme in man's literature, had motivated the New World's earliest explorers from Ponce de León onward. Constantine Panunzio, in his recollections, reiterated Adamic's pull of adventure. For Panunzio, the freedom of the West and "the call of the sea was in my very soul," he wrote. "Two things only" he "seemed able to picture: the vast stretches of virgin lands and the great, winding rivers. I had read something of the

Indians. . . . I got the idea that America was a . . . great country, vast in its proportions, vaguely beautiful." The myth that the American West represented a "Garden of the World" appeared early in the immigrant mentality, a state of mind that stimulated immigration. "Among the hundreds of myths cherished by the peasants," writes Carlo Levi, "one stands out among the rest by providing the perfect avenue of escape from grim realities. . . . It is their version, magical and real at the same time, of an earthly paradise, lost and then found again: the myth of America." Immigrants coupled the myth of the primeval with a rising level of expectation at home. Levi points out that, as early as 1853, the villagers of Vasto, a town in the Abruzzi region, protested deforestation of their land and threatened, because of the danger to "our pastures," to emigrate to California. . . .

The Migration Begins

From 1860 to 1870 only 12,000 Italians left their homeland for the United States. Italy's agricultural depression of 1887, however, made unemployment acute; decreasing the need for farm hands, it markedly stepped up expatriation. By then Italy had an excess of births over deaths of 350,000 per year. By 1906, despite heavy emigration, there was still an annual surplus of eleven per thousand persons in births over deaths. In the years of this century before the First World War, 8,500,0000 Italians emigrated abroad. Although some 2,400,000 of them later returned home, a net total immigration of over 6,000,000 persons occurred at a time when Italy's population consisted of only 35,000,000 persons. Most Italian emigrants arrived in the United States in the years from 1880 to 1924, during one of the greatest—and last—waves of immigration of all times. As they sought new moorings in a promised land, a veritable emigration fever gripped these masses.

The majority of Italians en route to America came from the countryside and had not seen a major city before reaching embarkation points. After 1880, the ports of Genoa, Naples, and Palermo became great human expatriation centers. To discourage vast crowds from milling about these ports, steamship companies were forbidden to advertise more than the bare details of sailing dates. Across the ocean, as many as fifteen thousand Italians reached Ellis Island in a single day. In 1880 steerage passenger rates from Naples to New York were only $15.00; they grew to $28.00 by 1900.

The federal census of 1900 recorded that since 1820 (no immigration records were kept before that date) some 20,000,000 newcomers had entered the United States and that one-third of the nation consisted of foreign-born residents or the children of foreign-born. United States immigration reached its crest in 1907, when 1,285,000 foreigners arrived. For years, the annual number of arrivals from abroad passed the million mark. From 1900 to 1914 13,500,000 immigrants came to America. In 1901 alone half a million persons left Italy. In the single year 1913, one person in forty departed from that country.

Italian-born persons would one day become the second-largest foreign element in the United States. In 1910 the federal census counted 1,343,000 Italians here. With their native-born children, they numbered that year well over 2,000,000 persons. In the following decade another 1,109,524 appeared. They forged a living link between their homeland and America as millions of Italians flowed into United States ports.

An Italian Immigrant's Aspirations

Rocco Corresca

Most Italian immigrants to the United States left Italy to escape lives of hopeless poverty, and Rocco Corresca was no exception. His earliest memory was of being taken from an orphanage by an old man who claimed he was Rocco's grandfather. The man immediately put Rocco to work begging on the streets. Rocco and his friend Francesco ran away and were taken in by a kindly fisherman named Ciguciano and his daughter Teresa. The two boys heard about opportunities in America and decided to emigrate from their homeland. In this selection, Rocco describes the boys' passage by ship to America and their immediate encounter with a padrone, a person who arranged for immigrants to become contract laborers. The padrone exploited the two boys for nearly a year before Rocco and Francesco broke away to establish their own business as bootblacks. Rocco's story was first published in 1906 in a collection of interviews edited by Hamilton Holt entitled *The Life Stories of {Undistinguished} Americans as Told by Themselves*. When the interview was conducted, Rocco was nineteen, owned his own business, and had managed to save a substantial amount of money.

Now and then I had heard things about America—that it was a far-off country where everybody was rich and that Italians went there and made plenty of money, so that they could return to Italy and live in pleasure ever after. One

Rocco Corresca, "The Life Story of an Italian Bootblack," *The Life Stories of {Undistinguished} Americans as Told by Themselves*, edited by Hamilton Holt, with a new introduction by Werner Sollors. New York: Routledge, 1990. Copyright © 1990 by Routledge, Chapman and Hall, Inc. All rights reserved. Reproduced by permission of Routledge/Taylor & Francis Books, Inc., and the author.

day I met a young man who pulled out a handful of gold and told me he had made that in America in a few days.

I said I should like to go there, and he told me that if I went he would take care of me and see that I was safe. I told Francesco [a childhood friend] and he wanted to go, too. So we said good-bye to our good friends. Teresa [a friend] cried and kissed us both and the priest came and shook our hands and told us to be good men, and that no matter where we went God and his saints were always near us and that if we lived well we should all meet again in heaven. We cried, too, for it was our home, that place. Ciguciano [a fisherman who befriended him] gave us money and slapped us on the back and said that we should be great. But he felt bad, too, at seeing us go away after all that time.

The young man took us to a big ship and got us work away down where the fires are. We had to carry coal to the place where it could be thrown on the fires. Francesco and I were very sick from the great heat at first and lay on the coal for a long time, but they threw water on us and made us get up. We could not stand on our feet well, for every- thing was going around and we had no strength. We said that we wished we had stayed in Italy no matter how much gold there was in America. We could not eat for three days and could not do much work. Then we got better and some- times we went up above and looked about. There was no land anywhere and we were much surprised. How could the people tell where to go when there was no land to steer by?

We were so long on the water that we began to think we should never get to America or that, perhaps, there was not any such place, but at last we saw land and came up to New York.

The Padrone

We were glad to get over without giving money, but I have heard since that we should have been paid for our work among the coal and that the young man who had sent us got money for it. We were all landed on an island and the bosses there said that Francesco and I must go back because we had not enough money, but a man named Bartolo came up and told them that we were brothers and he was our uncle and would take care of us. He brought two other men who swore that they knew us in Italy and that Bartolo was our uncle. I had never seen any of them before, but even then Bartolo might be my uncle, so I did not say anything. The bosses of the island let us go out with Bartolo after he had made the oath.

We came to Brooklyn, New York, to a wooden house in Adams street that was full of Italians from Naples. Bartolo had a room on the third floor and there were fifteen men in the room, all boarding with Bartolo. He did the cooking on

Italian immigrants endured a long Atlantic crossing in hopes of starting a new, prosperous life in America.

a stove in the middle of the room and there were beds all around the sides, one bed above another. It was very hot in the room, but we were soon asleep, for we were very tired.

The next morning, early, Bartolo told us to go out and pick rags and get bottles. He gave us bags and hooks and showed us the ash barrels. On the streets where the fine houses are the people are very careless and put out good things, like mattresses and umbrellas, clothes, bats and boots. We brought all these to Bartolo and he made them new again and sold them on the sidewalk; but mostly we brought rags and bones. The rags we had to wash in the back yard and then we hung them to dry on lines under the ceiling in our room. The bones we kept under the beds till Bartolo could find a man to buy them.

Most of the men in our room worked at digging the sewer. Bartolo got them the work and they paid him about one-quarter of their wages. Then he charged them for board and he bought the clothes for them, too. So they got little money after all.

Bartolo was always saying that the rent of the room was so high that he could not make anything, but he was really making plenty. He was what they call a padrone and is now a very rich man. The men that were living with him had just come to the country and could not speak English. They had all been sent by the young man we met in Italy. Bartolo told us all that we must work for him and that if we did not the police would come and put us in prison.

He gave us very little money, and our clothes were some of those that were found on the street. Still we had enough to eat and we had meat quite often, which we never had in Italy. Bartolo got it from the butcher—the meat that he could not sell to the other people—but it was quite good meat. Bartolo cooked it in the pan while we all sat on our beds in the evening. Then he cut it into small bits and passed the pan around, saying:

"See what I do for you and yet you are not glad. I am too kind a man, that is why I am so poor."

We were with Bartolo nearly a year, but some of our countrymen who had been in the place a long time said that Bartolo had no right to us and we could get work for a dollar and a half a day, which, when you make it *lire* (reckoned in the Italian currency) is very much. So we went away one day to Newark and got work on the street. Bartolo came after us and make a great noise, but the boss said that if he did not go away soon the police would have him. Then he went, saying that there was no justice in this country. . . .

The Bootblack Business

When the Newark boss told us that there was no more work Francesco and I talked about what we would do and we went back to Brooklyn to a saloon near Hamilton Ferry where we got a job cleaning it out and slept in a little room upstairs. There was a bootblack named Michael on the corner and when I had time I helped him and learned the business. Francesco cooked the lunch in the saloon and he, too, worked for the bootblack and we were soon able to make the best polish.

Then we thought we would go into business and we got a basement on Hamilton avenue, near the Ferry, and put four chairs in it. We paid $75 for the chairs and all the other things. We had tables and looking glasses there and curtains. We took the papers that have the pictures in and made the place high toned. Outside we had a big sign that said:

THE BEST SHINE FOR TEN CENTS

Men that did not want to pay 10¢ could get a good shine for 5¢ but it was not an oil shine. We had two boys helping us and paid each of them 50¢ a day. The rent of the place was $20 a month, so the expenses were very great, but we made money from the beginning. We slept in the basement, but got our meals in the saloon till we could put a stove in our place, and then Francesco cooked for us all. That would not do, though, because some of our customers said that they did not like to smell garlic and onions and red herrings. I thought that was strange, but we had to do what the customers said. So we got the woman who lived upstairs to give us our meals and paid her $1.50 a week each. She gave the boys soup in the middle of the day—5¢ for two plates. . . .

Deciding to Stay in America

We had said that when we saved $1,000 each we would go back to Italy and buy a farm, but now that the time is coming we are so busy and making so much money that we think we will stay. We have opened another parlor near South Ferry, in New York. We have to pay $30 a month rent, but the business is very good. The boys in this place charge 60¢ a day because there is so much work.

At first we did not know much of this country, but by and by we learned. There are here plenty of Protestants who are heretics, but they have a religion, too. Many of the finest churches are Protestant, but they have no saints and no altars, which seems strange.

These people are without a king such as ours in Italy. It is what they call a Republic, as [Italian statesman] Garibaldi wanted, and every year in the fall the people vote. They wanted us to vote last fall, but we did not. A man came and said that he would get us made Americans for 50¢ and then we could get $2 for our votes. I talked to some of our people and they told me that we should have to put a paper in a box telling who we wanted to govern us.

I went with five men to the court and when they asked me how long I had been in the country I told them two years. Afterward my countrymen said I was a fool and would never learn politics.

"You should have said you were five years here and then we would swear to it," was what they told me.

I and Francesco are to be Americans in three years. The court gave us papers and said we must wait and we must be able to read some things and tell who the ruler of the country is.

There are plenty of rich Italians here, men who a few years ago had nothing and now have so much money that they could not count all their dollars in a week. The richest ones go away from the other Italians and live with the Americans.

We have joined a club and have much pleasure in the evenings. The club has rooms down in Sackett street and we meet many people and are learning new things all the time. We were very ignorant when we came here, but now we have learned much.

On Sundays we get a horse and carriage from the grocer and go down to Coney Island. We go to the theaters often, and other evenings we go to the houses of our friends and play cards.

I am now nineteen years of age and have $700 saved. Francesco is twenty-one and has about $900. We shall open some more parlors soon. I know an Italian who was a bootblack ten years ago and now bosses bootblacks all over the city, who has so much money that if it was turned into gold it would weigh more than himself.

Francesco and I have a room to ourselves and some people call us "swells." Ciguciano said that we should be great men. Francesco bought a gold watch with a gold chain as thick as his thumb. He is a very handsome fellow and I think he likes a young lady that he met at a picnic out at Ridgewood.

I often think of Ciguciano and Teresa. He is a good man, one in a thousand, and she was very beautiful. Maybe I shall write to them about coming to this country.

Life in America's Urban Slums

Michael La Sorte

Italian immigrants usually left their homeland because of the extreme poverty they faced there. America offered the promise of a more prosperous future. However, conditions in the new country were far from perfect. In addition to performing long hours of low-paid backbreaking labor, Italian immigrants were forced by poverty and racism to live in urban slums with poor housing and inadequate sanitation. In this selection from his book *La Merica: Images of Italian Greenhorn Experience*, Michael La Sorte describes the slums of lower Manhattan in New York City and in Boston's North End. Italian families there tried to improve living conditions by establishing boardinghouses and by renting rooms to bachelor Italian immigrants. Italian housewives ran the boardinghouses while their husbands held outside jobs. Italian laborers working on the railroads and in construction suffered the worst living conditions. They often lived in shanties and railroad boxcars and were usually treated with contempt by their American employers. La Sorte is a professor of sociology at the University of New York at Brockport.

In the 1870s the Italian community in lower Manhattan began to spread beyond lower Mulberry Street. The Italians took over Hester and Mott Streets from the Irish, gradually replaced them on Baxter Street, and spilled over into upper Mulberry. By 1880 there were 20,000 Italians living

Michael La Sorte, *La Merica: Images of Italian Greenhorn Experience*. Philadelphia: Temple University Press, 1985. Copyright © 1985 by Temple University. All rights reserved. Reproduced by permission.

in the Mulberry Street area, on Eleventh Street, uptown in Yorkville, and across the Hudson River in Hoboken. They occupied some of the poorest housing in the city. The notorious Five Points section of lower Manhattan was referred to jokingly as the "Boulevard des Italians," thus discrediting the Italians by associating them in the public's mind with the creation of the worst slum in New York.

The thousands of Italians who moved into Five Points, crowding others who had been there for decades, lived in filth and squalor, working as shoeshine boys, organ grinders, garbagemen, and rag collectors. These people had known the chronic poverty of the Italian countryside, but even the stark misery of the most desolate mountain village of Basilicata could barely compete with what awaited them in New York. In 1879, Adolfo Rossi wandered through these streets several times, marveling at the tenacity of the inhabitants and their ability to survive in an environment poorer than most barnyard animals enjoyed. A sense of total alienation and hopelessness so gripped the population that, whenever possible, men and women would descend to one of the many subterranean bars to drink themselves into a stupor on overpriced rotgut. Angelo Mosso, in 1905, was appalled by what his countrymen had to endure as immigrants. "It is a sad spectacle seeing tens of thousands of famished people as collectors of animal and human refuse. The ugly, overcrowded tenements in which they reside must harbor every conceivable infection." Marginati was shocked by the filth and misery of Mott and Mulberry Streets. The entire Italian colony, he said, was not worth "the price the small amount of dynamite needed to blow it up." Franco Ciarlantini on the other hand was entranced by the pace and style of life among the New York Italians. He found a certain exotic charm in the slum existence, describing the Italian colony as emitting "a babble of sounds, a variety of odors. The tone is set most of all by the children, who are everywhere. They dominate the streets, the squares, the parks, incontestably. The streets are full of color, of contrasts, of festivity."

Immigrant housing in other major cities was also rude and primitive. Gaetano Conte was struck most by the density of Boston's North End tenement population, where 85 percent of the Italians lived in the 1890s. Ciarlantini's "variety of odors" was for Conte an "unsupportable stench," particularly noticeable on a sweltering summer day. The smells were nauseating, the vermin omnipresent, and the cleaning facilities scanty. There was no escape from the rot and decay of the housing and the suffocating pressure of people. The poorest Italians lived huddled together in miserable apartments, covered with filth and dressed in rags. Their diet consisted largely of stale bread, stale fruit, and stale beer. The rents far exceeded the quality of the apartments. Back rooms with little or no natural light, renting for $1.75 to $2.50 a month, were occupied by whole families or by a number of male lodgers. Three or four slept to a bed. To the outsider, the North End was a dusty, dirty, and mysterious place, considered dangerous after dark. . . .

The Italian Boardinghouse

The Italians did not live alone; single-person households were very rare. One characteristic arrangement for unattached male immigrant workers was the large boardinghouse. These were sometimes found in the large cities, but more often they were established in quasi-rural locations near the work sites. Such houses were usually operated by an Italian hostler who was sometimes also the Boss of the men who lived there. They ranged from households of a dozen boarders to hotel-type arrangements with 30 to 50 residents. The Boss had either brought the men over from

Italy or recruited them to work for him after their arrival, or he was acting as their hiring agent. Most of the money that such workers earned went to the Boss for food and lodging. There were few amenities: living space was at a premium, and the men did their own cooking. . . .

The most common type of living arrangement in the Italian colonies was the nuclear family household: a man, his wife and their children, and frequently a few unrelated boarders—in some cases as many as ten—most of them between the ages of 15 to 40. Such an arrangement became a necessity for the large proportion of men who arrived in America alone, without their families. (The pattern had a relatively short life span, perhaps no more than three or four decades; it disappeared after the First World War with the dwindling of worker immigration and the return to Italy or the formation of their own nuclear families of those who had been boarders.) Without Italian families to take them in, there would have been few places for these worker immigrants to live. Only a handful of Italians boarded in non-Italian households. A review of the 1900 Federal census manuscripts for upstate New York reveals that there were only two Italians boarding with families not Italian in origin. Few Italians, particularly the new arrivals, had a desire to live with foreigners who did not speak their language or cook their food, nor were they welcome to do so. American boardinghouses frequently made the sentiment explicit with signs reading, "We do not rent to Negroes or Italians."

The ideal arrangement was to live with one's own *paesani* [countrymen], and *paesani* were usually preferred as boarders. Totonno [an Italian immigrant] was not successful in persuading his Boss to accept a non-*paesano* friend of his as a boarder, even though the man came from a village only a few kilometers from their own. There were good reasons for such a decision. Mixed Italian boardinghouses created problems: regional differences were often too glaring to be overlooked, and daily friction was predictable. Totonno wanted to move away from his *paesani* because they were "suffocating" him, but he found that other Italians were worse. Margariti lived in a number of mixed boardinghouses; there was violence in each one. He soon realized that to live a peaceful existence, he had to remain with other Calabresi like himself.

It was common practice for the head of a household to board any man who was working for him. The boarder would take part in the life of the family, its fortunes and misfortunes; he ate at the family table and was in all respects treated like a dependent member of the family. As an example, the Barbieri family (selected at random from the 1900 Federal census manuscripts) lived at 162 Hartford Street in Rochester, New York. The head of the household, Frank Barbieri, a pianomaker, was born in 1854 and emigrated in 1882 at age 28. In 1884 his wife Mary, then 27 years old, and their infant daughter joined him. The next four children, ages 14, 11, 8, and 6, were born in Canada and the last two, ages 5 and 1, in New York state. In addition, there were two single male boarders; one man worked for Frank, and the other was a day laborer.

Because taking in boarders meant additional income for the family, two or three men might be accommodated even if it meant considerably more housework and congested quarters. Typically, the husband and wife would give one or two rooms over to the boarders, while they and their children slept together in the master bedroom.

Women's Work

The woman of the house sometimes had the responsibility of ministering to the needs of a large number of men. Not only did she wash and cook for her own boarders, but often on Sundays, a day for socializing, men who were boarding elsewhere and did not enjoy good cooking during the week would also be at the table. At large festive dinners, several women would contribute to the meal.

Arrangements between the boarder and the housekeeper varied. She might do all his housekeeping chores for a specified sum, or the boarder might pay for each service as it was rendered. In some cases, the boarders purchased their own foodstuffs, and the woman would place the goods, carefully labeled, in a cupboard or on a shelf above the stove. Then each man would let her know when he left in the morning what he wanted for dinner that evening, and she would have each dish prepared when the men arrived from work. One man would have spaghetti, another liver, a third pork ribs and cabbage or the popular sausages and peppers. Those men who were down on their luck might satisfy themselves with an inexpensive but filling vegetable stew or some other simple dish without meat.

Rosa Mondari was one of these women who spent much of her life providing for immigrant boarders. Rosa came to the American West in 1908 as a young bride of 18 years of age. She cooked and washed for dozens of miners in addition to raising her four children and caring for her husband. She would arise before dawn, prepare an early breakfast for the men, pack their lunches, and cook them a big meal in the evening. She took her job seriously and was interested in keeping the men content. "The man who works hard must eat well," she believed. "A good dinner is his only comfort." Rosa, and others like her, had been raised in the Old World tradition of household servility and accepted her role as mistress of the house, a person who established high standards both for herself and her boarders. In the house, she ruled; the men would refer to her as *La Signora* or *La Bossa* or *La Padrona*. . . .

The worst living conditions were endured by the work gangs. Throughout the late 1800s and early 1900s, countless thousands of Italians were hired to labor in lumber camps, on road construction, and on the railroads in various parts of the United States. Because there were rarely any civilized amenities in these areas and because they moved frequently from one work site to another, these immigrants lived in the most primitive fashion. There were no women to take care of the domestic chores; the men labored a full day and also had to do their own cooking and cleaning, and sometimes had to construct their own living quarters. The tales that have come out of these work gangs reveal that the men were brutally exploited by those who hired and commanded them, that they were little more than chattel, and that they lived under conditions that were demonstrably worse than those they had left behind in Italy. Outside of Rome, New York, one hot July day in 1913, Totonno encountered a road gang cooking a meal outside the tumbledown shanty they had constructed. Totonno was shocked by the way these men "chose" to live. Their clothes were little more than rags, they were indescribably filthy from the ever-present road dust, their bodies were emaciated, and they were totally spiritless. It was a depressing spectacle for Totonno, who was ashamed that his countrymen would allow themselves to be reduced to so subhuman a level. . . .

To the railroad companies, boxcars were ideal dormitories for the crews. Cars that had been abandoned or retired from active service cost nothing to maintain and, if still mobile, could be easily moved as the job progressed along the line. The men who lived in these cars never forgot the experience. [Francesco] Ventresca, who worked on a section gang in upstate New York, called life in the boxcars a "compact existence." Along the Cumberland Railroad in West Virginia, Pasquale D'Angelo slept on boards over which dirty straw was strewn: "The creaking and cracked floor was covered with straw which had fallen from the wooden

shelves where we slept. The whole inside . . . with its for-
lorn occupants gave a picture of moral wreck and bitter-
ness. We were pigs in our sty." The boxcar [Carmine] Ian-
nace occupied in Pennsylvania contained no straw for fear
that it would ignite. The Sardinians in the car found the
bare boards comfortable; they had never known a bed. Ian-
nace awoke each morning stiff, cold, and exhausted. . . .

The foremen, the timekeepers, and the other railway employees, most of whom were American or Americanized
immigrants, kept their social distance from the laborers,
whom they considered to be loafers and ingrates. The railroad companies carefully selected the toughest and mean-
est foremen, individuals who were willing to do the railroad's bidding for a little more pay and who could obtain
from the workers their last ounce of effort. There was no
desire to improve the living conditions of the men, because
workers were thought not to have sensibilities. "Those
workers are beasts," the foreman told [Domenick] Ciolli.
"They must not be given a rest, otherwise they will step all
over me." He sold the Italians stale and moldy bread at nine
cents a loaf: "Take that, you pigs," he would tell them, "you
never had better bread at home." The workers, the foreman
insisted, did not deserve any better than they were getting.
The American timekeeper was in full agreement; when the
men complained about intolerable conditions, the timekeeper dismissed their complaints as unfounded. "These
dagoes are never satisfied," he told Ciolli. "If they are given
a finger they will take the entire hand. They should be
starved to death. They don't belong here."

The Italians in Northern California

Jerre Mangione and Ben Morreale

Although the majority of Italian immigrants ended their journey in the cities of America's Northeast, others dispersed throughout the continental United States. California was especially appealing to immigrants because of the rumors of gold, productive agricultural land, and natural beauty. In this selection from their book *La Storia: Five Centuries of the Italian American Experience*, authors Jerre Mangione and Ben Morreale trace the history of Italian immigrants in northern California during the nineteenth and early twentieth centuries. After the Italian immigrants realized that the best gold-mining claims had already been taken by American prospectors, they became successful entrepreneurs in the fishing industry and in wine production. Others became involved in banking and finance. Mangione, who died in 1998, also wrote a memoir of Italian American life called *Mount Allegro*. Morreale, a professor of history at State University of New York at Plattsburgh, has written several fiction and nonfiction books about Italians, including *Sicily: The Hallowed Land* and *Italian Americans: The Immigrant Experience* (with coauthor Robert Carola).

The image of American streets paved with gold may have struck Italians for the first time in 1848, when gold was discovered at Sutters Sawmill near San Francisco, a city named by Spaniards to honor one of Italy's favorite saints.

Jerre Mangione and Ben Morreale, *La Storia: Five Centuries of the Italian American Experience*. New York: HarperPerennial, A Division of HarperCollins Publishers, Aaron Asher Books, 1993. Copyright © 1992 by Jerre Mangione and Ben Morreale. All rights reserved. Reproduced by permission of HarperCollins Publishers, Inc.

Among those hit with gold fever were several hundred Italians from northern Italy. Some came after wandering through South America and the southwestern states. Italian sailors on board ships bringing Carrara marble to San Francisco jumped ship to join the gold seekers. The pioneers also included Italian farm laborers and fishermen who came directly from Italy, after hearing from unscrupulous steamship agents that in California they could pluck gold rocks from the nooks and crevices "with their bare hands and a knife."

Most arrived too late to stake out claims in the most desirable sites and had to travel far beyond Sutters Sawmill to find unclaimed areas. Wherever they went, the Italians encountered American prospectors guarding their claims. Suspicion and greed resulted in shootings, knifings, and fistfights. Also discouraging to the Italians was the reality that, though they worked steadily from early morning until dark, they gained little more than sore muscles for their efforts. Many soon shelved their dreams of quick riches and looked elsewhere, abandoning mining for more stable and familiar occupations such as farming.

Italians in San Francisco

Many of the Italians settled in the fertile Sacramento-San Joaquin Valley. Others drifted north, as far as Oregon and Washington, to work in lumber camps, coal mines, and vineyards. Still others returned to San Francisco, where they worked for other Italians who, unmoved by gold fever, catered to the city's growing foreign population with restaurants, boardinghouses, groceries, and clothing stores. The California economy, especially in San Francisco, flourished in the Gold Rush era. By 1870, San Francisco's population numbered 149,000, half of whom were foreign-born. Of these, only 1,600 were Italians; 50 years later the Italians were the leading immigrant group, comprising 20 percent of all foreign-born residents.

The Italians in San Francisco settled first around Telegraph Hill, a rocky bluff 300 feet high stretching down to the waterfront and reminiscent of a Mediterranean seaside village. The Irish, first to arrive, lived at the top of the hill; the Germans were in the middle; and at the base, where the rents were cheapest and access to the fishing boats quickest, were the Italians. A ditty of the time put it this way:

> The Irish they lived on the top av it,
> And the Dagos they lived at the bas av it,
> And the goats and the chicks and the brickbats
> And Shticks
> Is joombled all over th' face of it . . .

The Italian settlement grew, displacing the Germans and the Irish. As more Italians arrived, they moved into the North Beach district adjacent to the Hill. The combined section became known as the Latin Quarter, and later as the Italian Quarter, where not a sign was printed or written in English. At first the Italian settlers were mostly fishermen and farmers, but as the immigration from Italy increased in the early twentieth century, their ranks included laborers, artisans, mechanics, shopkeepers, and restaurant owners. Those intent on farming (mainly Neapolitans, Ligurians, and Tuscans) gravitated to the Outer Mission district, where they worked together to turn sandy dunes into productive acres, specializing in lettuce and artichokes.

The Italians in the Telegraph Hill enclave maintained many of their native customs, one of which may have saved the quarter from complete disaster during the 1906 earthquake. When quake fires began to creep up the Hill, the residents rolled barrels of wine from their cellars and, forming a bucket brigade, succeeded in protecting their houses from the flames with blankets soaked in the wine.

Although it was assumed that most Italians in San Francisco came from northern Italy, the anthropologist Paul Radin in a government-sponsored study revealed that 36 percent came from southern Italy, 10 percent from central Italy, and 54 percent from northern Italy.

As in many other states, the early San Francisco immigrants were mostly Genovesi and Tuscans; later arrivals hailed from Calabria, Campania, and Sicily. Most came directly from Italy, via New York, where they had boarded the transcontinental train to San Francisco. Railroad agents promised good wages and cheap land in California, and the immigrants paid from $110 to $120 for their fares to a place where they were assured they could recoup that investment within a few weeks. Many arrived during a period of national economic crisis and high unemployment which provoked gangs of unemployed men, such as Coxey's Army in 1894[1] to march on Washington demanding relief. The new immigrants were not welcomed by their Italian compatriots, who disparaged them for their lack of skills and feared that the discrimination often practiced by American employers against southern Italians, especially after the New Orleans lynchings,[2] might be extended to them. Eventually, the newcomers found jobs as fishermen, farmhands, garbage collectors, and in canning factories, usually among the *paesani* [countrymen] from their home villages who had preceded them.

The Fishing Industry

There was intense competition between southerners and northerners in agriculture and fishing, which extended over a period of years, with the Sicilians finally winning control of the fishing industry by the first decade of the century. . . .

1. a group of unemployed men who marched on Washington, D.C., during a depression to demand work   2. Eleven Italians were lynched by a mob in 1891 after being tried and released for the murder of the chief of police.

In the Bay area the fishermen were especially conspicuous. Sundays, as they and their families gathered in the morning to repair nets and boats as was the custom in the small fishing villages around Palermo, they sang folk songs and operatic arias while they worked. In good weather they would board their boats and picnic on the shores of Marin County. For all of the immigrant families, their two-hour Sunday meal was the highlight of the day. After dinner, the women would chat and sew while the men sat in Washington Square or went to the social club of *paesani* to which they belonged and played cards. Sunday afternoons were also reserved for *bocce* teams, which competed at Fisherman's Wharf. The Tuscans had their own favorite sport, *pallone*, which was played on empty lots with wheels of Tuscan cheese. A leather strap was placed around a wheel of *Pecorino* and sent rolling. The winner was the player who could send it the farthest along a straight line. The audience, as well as the players themselves, bet with one another, and the player who won got the cheese and whatever bets he had made. One of the few annual events that attracted San Franciscans of all nationalities was Discoverer's Day—one of the first events in the nation dedicated to Christopher Columbus. Following church services there was a lengthy parade to the Municipal Pier, the site of the explorer's statue.

North Beach grew into San Francisco's dominant Italian enclave after 1900, as more men sent for their families. In North Beach and Washington Square in particular, the immigrants could recapture the memory of their native village with its *piazza*, the outdoor social center of the community. Another gathering spot was Fisherman's Wharf, which on Sundays became picnic grounds for fishermen and their families. The most popular of the festivals were staged annually by the fishermen, Sicilians paying homage to the Madonna of Porticello (an area near Palermo noted for its swordfish) during "the blessing of the fleet," whose boats were painted blue and white for the occasion.

Fisherman's Wharf served as the harbor for 700 fishing vessels, which averaged a daily catch of 11,500 tons. The Genovesi were the first Italians to dominate the industry, which they did by driving away the Greeks and Slovaks. The Italians introduced two pieces of fishing equipment they had known in Europe which gave them distinct advantage over their competitors: the *paranzella*, a trawling net that was dragged over the fishing grounds; and the *felucca*, a small, shallow vessel specially built to withstand high winds and rough water. The *felucca* permitted as many as a half dozen men to spend two or three days at a time fishing. The vessel was easily identifiable by its colorful triangular sail, denoting the native region of its fishermen. . . .

Agriculture and Banking

One of the most enterprising Genovesi in the area was Andrea Sbarbaro, who founded the first building and loan association in San Francisco. He also established a night school for fishermen and their children in the North Beach area. An idealist who had been influenced by [Russian writer Leo] Tolstoy and [Italian nationalist Giuseppe] Mazzini, Sbarbaro organized a cooperative in the Sonoma Valley known as the Italian-Swiss Agricultural Colony (so named because there was a Swiss on its board of directors), which hired peasants who had worked in the Italian vineyards. Sbarbaro paid them fair wages, provided them with all the wine they could drink, and offered them shares in the cooperative. The shares, originally worth $135,000, were valued at $3 million by 1910. Italian Swiss Colony became one of the earliest American wineries able to market its wine products nationally.

If Sbarbaro saved the Colony, it was Pietro Carlo Rossi who made it prosper. Rossi, a winemaster from Asti, Piedmont, improved the quality of the wine and attracted world attention by winning the Grand Prix for his wines at an international congress held in Turin. He also provided seasonal employment for area families.

If the gold-lined streets of California turned out to be a myth, Amadeo Pietro Giannini did his best to make it a reality in San Francisco.

Giannini—future founder and chairman of the Bank of America—was born of immigrant parents from Genoa in 1870 and began his career as a fruit peddler. Giannini opened the Bank of Italy in 1904 with capital from his stepfather and a few friends. He solicited deposits and loans door to door for farmers, laborers, and small merchants.

During the great San Francisco earthquake of 1906, Giannini harnessed two horses to a wagon and rushed to his bank, through burning streets filled with looters and drunks, to rescue $2 million in gold and securities. His was the only bank open for business (housed temporarily in a waterfront shed) when the fires burned out. From then on, Giannini's rise in the banking world was spectacular. In 1919, he innovated the branch banking system. In 1928, he formed Transamerica Corporation, a holding company for all his financial enterprises; by 1930, it had become the Bank of America. By 1945 the Bank of America was the world's largest private bank, with more than 3 million depositors, $6 million in resources, and 495 branches.

Giannini never lost his (in the eyes of other bankers) eccentric concern for the small man, lending money to fruit growers, small merchants, and laborers on their signatures alone. He was the first to finance filmmakers, Charles Chaplin, Mack Sennett, and Darryl Zanuck among them. At seventy-five Giannini, a *faitature* (fighter), as the immigrants might have called him, retired to live with his daughter, "to swim, to listen to music," until his death in 1949.

Italians Try to Preserve Their Traditions in Oklahoma

Kenny L. Brown

Although the majority of Italian immigrants found a home in the urban centers of America's Northeast, many dispersed throughout the country to the fisheries and vineyards of northern California, to the mines of Colorado, and to the business district of New Orleans, Louisiana. The coal mines in the Indian territory that would become the state of Oklahoma in 1907 attracted Italian immigrants as well, and an Italian enclave formed in that area in the last decade of the nineteenth and first decade of the twentieth centuries. In the next selection, Kenny L. Brown argues that the Italians of eastern Oklahoma were slower to assimilate into American society than their compatriots living in multicultural urban centers. He describes the traditions that the early Italian immigrants held onto—particularly the customs of courtship and marriage. Eventually, however, Italian families were transformed as subsequent generations adopted American customs. Brown is a professor of history at the University of Central Oklahoma and is the author of many books and articles about Oklahoma history.

Probably one of the most important changes that took place in the [immigrant] Italians' lives was the inevitable transformation and Americanization of the family unit. In Italy the peasant family was patriarchal—a well-defined

Kenny L. Brown, *The Italians in Oklahoma*. Norman: University of Oklahoma Press, 1980. Copyright © 1980 by the University of Oklahoma Press, Norman, Publishing Division of the University. Reproduced by permission.

unit with the father as head and with every member having a strong sense of responsibility for the other members of the family. The father not only assigned the chores and responsibilities to the children but also provided the family with necessities. He was seldom disputed in a decision concerning the family. The eldest son and mother advised the father, however, and had at least some power in the decision-making process.

Family Relationships

In Italy the woman acknowledged her husband as family head; yet she carried out certain duties that were no less important. The mother took charge of rearing the children, insuring their religious instruction, and preparing them for marriage. She also articulated the social relations of the family. The children were particularly obedient largely because of the severe punishment that they received when they chose to defy their parents. They were taught to have a strong regard for the family, and they usually considered the effect on the whole family before making a personal decision.

A vast majority of the Italians who came to the United States settled in large cities such as New York where the traditions of the family were greatly altered. The father, working in a factory, had less contact with and less control over the family. The Italian mother often worked in a garment shop and lost much authority over the children, though she also gained a new sense of autonomy because of her new contacts outside the family. Further altering the family structure in the American cities was the new independence of the children who became more rebellious as they made acquaintances with a large number of children in their neighborhoods. If the family unit deteriorated, it was largely because of the distance between the parents and children.

In Oklahoma the situation differed substantially. The coal-mining area did not present the same problems as the urban areas. The patriarchal family unit remained an accepted way of life to most of the immigrants as well as Americans in the rural and small-town atmosphere. Few of the conflicts with tradition existed in Oklahoma as they did in the eastern cities where the family unit easily deteriorated. The father of the Italian family in Oklahoma retained much of his authority. During territorial days the children had little opportunity to go to school, and some parents, particularly southern Italians, sometimes deliberately kept the children from going to school. Many parents also insisted that the children speak only Italian at home; as a result, many children had little chance to learn English and assimilation was slow in the early days.

Women and Women's Work

If any member of the Italian family in Oklahoma was slow to change, it was the immigrant woman. Because the Italians lived in colonies, the women had little cause to associate with people other than those of their own nationalistic background. Unlike the large cities in other parts of the country, there were no factories where Italian women could work and find a certain degree of independence from their husbands. Even domestic service was not available in the area, for only a small number of people could afford maids or household servants. If their husbands owned businesses, the Italian wives sometimes worked as clerks or assistants, but this was not frequent. Otherwise, the only consequential economic activity, involving about one-fourth of the Italian women in Oklahoma, was the providing of rooms and service for boarders. Since mostly Italian men took the rooms, renting did not bring many Italian women into contact with those outside their nationality.

The immigrant Italian women in Oklahoma, virtually

isolated from contact with the larger community, had lives that were centered on the home. Very few Italian women over twenty years of age were unmarried, and the daily routine and tasks were much like those undertaken by American women in other rural areas or small towns in the late nineteenth and early twentieth centuries. Clothes were washed by hand or on a rubboard, and cheese and sausage were made at home for the family. Most Italian women baked their own bread. Almost every backyard had a stone or brick oven that the wife heated once or twice a week to cook twenty to thirty loaves. Sometimes neighbors would undertake these household tasks jointly, particularly if a wife was ill or giving birth. Partially because of tradition and because of the slow transportation and lack of medical facilities, almost all Italian women gave birth to their children at home often attended only by midwives. Yet all was not hardship for Italian women. Sometimes when the men were at work, or more often on Sunday, the wives would meet, converse, cook, and crochet or embroider.

Most of the interactions among the Italian women were within their own group. Because only about one-fourth of the Italian women in the area could speak English and because most homes were conveniently located in an Italian colony, the Italian immigrant women relied on few things that were not Italian. There was even an Italian grocer in most neighborhoods who provided the necessary foodstuffs, often delivering items to each home. As a result, many Italian immigrant women of the area lived most of their lives in small communities, traded with Italian merchants, and never learned to speak English.

Although certain forces worked against the assimilation and Americanization of first-generation Italian women, their husbands and children came into contact with other forces that caused them to change. The coal mines and labor unions brought the men into contact with men of

other nationalities and with methods that were character-
istically American. Those Italian men who worked outside
of the mines often came into contact with American businessmen and were particularly changed because of it. With
the coming of statehood and compulsory education, the
children of the Italian immigrants were thrust into schools
where they inevitably changed due to contact with American children and the English language.

Courtship and Marriage

One part of the Italian culture that predominated was the
tradition of courtship and marriage. A few of the southern Italians continued to arrange marriages for their children as they had done in Italy, but this was not widespread. In many instances Italian bachelors wrote relatives
back home who selected a young woman and arranged a
marriage. Often the bride and groom had never met; sometimes the girl had been a childhood sweetheart.

For those young Italians who met, courted, and married
in Oklahoma, the customs and traditions of the old country were steadfastly observed. Fathers of Italian girls often
thwarted the designs of love-stricken young men. Only the
most respectable male suitors dared to call on young
women. Courtship was not a frivolous pastime, but was a
prelude to marriage.

Once a young woman's family gave permission for courtship, strict rules were followed. Almost all contact between
the unmarried man and woman was in the home of the
woman's parents. The couple was never alone since one or
more relatives attended the pair as they conversed and in-
teracted. Maria Finamore, a resident of Krebs, recalled
vividly this element of courtship: "For a while he sat in one
corner and I sat at the other corner and an uncle was in between us." Later in the courtship the couple was allowed to
take walks—with a chaperon. The unmarried young man

and woman could venture into public unattended only when they visited relatives and friends to announce their engagement and to extend invitations to the wedding.

Italian weddings in Oklahoma were usually large and joyous affairs. Most were held in the home of the parents of the bride or groom, and every relative of the extended family attended if possible. After a simple ceremony a celebration followed with plenty of food, drinks, and sometimes dancing. This type of wedding and the old rules for courtship lasted well into the 1930s. In later years, however, subsequent generations faced fewer restrictions on their courtships and more Americanized weddings.

Accusations Against Italian Immigrants

An Anonymous Writer to the *New York Times*

Many Americans felt threatened by the thousands of southern Italians who immigrated to the United States after 1880. The United States was suffering from periodic economic downturns, jobs were hard to find, and it was easy to point to the dark-skinned Sicilian laborers as the cause of all problems. Nativists, those Americans determined to preserve northern European immigration and culture in the United States, called for restrictions against the Italian immigrants who early on were branded as criminals. In fact, Italian immigrants themselves were being victimized in New York by a criminal gang called the Black Hand, so named because gang members left coal-blackened handprints on the doors of immigrants to intimidate them. A few of the Black Hand gang members belonged to the Sicilian Mafia, a self-protection society that sometimes engaged in criminal activity. However, most Black Hand members did not belong to the Mafia but were disenchanted Italian immigrants who saw thievery as more appealing than hard labor. The gang extorted money primarily from honest Italian immigrants, but in the minds of many Americans all Italian immigrants were perpetrators, not victims, of this criminal activity. News of the Mafia in Sicily reached American shores and soon the Black Hand, Mafia, and all Italians were lumped into the same category—all criminals. In this selection, an anonymous writer to the *New York Times* in 1884 accuses all Italians of being brigands (bandits and thieves). The writer spins out a scenario in which Italian immigrants are guilty of kidnapping and mutilation—a scenario that is totally imagined. The article

Anonymous, *New York Times*, January 1, 1884.

is now part of an anthology edited by Salvatore J. LaGumina that traces the history of discrimination against Italians in the United States. LaGumina, a professor at Nassau Community College in New York, is one of the founders of the American Italian Historical Association.

The case of Italian brigandage in Second-avenue seems to have startled timid people. Why should we not have Italian brigands? We have in this City some thirty thousand Italians, nearly all of whom came from the old Neapolitan Provinces, where, until recently, brigandage was the national industry. It is not strange that these immigrants should bring with them a fondness for their native pursuits. In the days of the Bourbons[1] brigandage was held to be a noble career, and the brigand ranked as high in popular estimation as our own railway wreckers rank with us. The Italians who come to this country with a hereditary respect for brigandage, and find that the men who are most talked of here are the Jesse Jameses [American robber] of the West and the Jay Goulds [wealthy entrepreneur] of the East, naturally think that there is a fine field in America for genuine Italian brigandage. The wonder is that they have ever thought of engaging in any other industry.

Capture and Ransom

New York City affords excellent opportunities for brigandage of the genuine Italian model. A band of brigands would find the rookeries of Mulberry street much more comfortable than the Calabrian forests, and much safer. The brigands, when pursued by the police, could pass from roof to roof, lie in ambush behind chimneys, defend narrow scuttles against a vastly superior force, and finally make their escape with much greater ease than could a

1. French rulers who controlled parts of Italy for a time

band surrounded in an Italian forest by a regiment of troops. When brigandage becomes fully organized here wealthy citizens will constantly be captured and held for ransom. Were Mr. Jay Gould, for example, to be seized by brigands, and confined in a Mulberry street cavern, they could demand, and perhaps obtain, half a million as his ransom. If the ransom was not promptly paid, an ear, a finger, or a nose neatly cut off and sent to his friends at regular intervals would stimulate them to action. Mr. Gould's nose alone is worth a large sum of money, as was established some years ago when it was pulled by an impulsive enemy, and Mr. Gould in the ensuing suit for damages estimated his nose to be worth something like $8,000. At this rate a very handsome sum could be obtained for Mr. Gould at retail, so to speak, and if his partner could succeed in finding the books of their firm, so as to make the necessary entry, they would undoubtedly prefer to ransom him whole, even for half a million, rather than to purchase him by installments. Perhaps even now the Italian quarters of the City have their bands of brigands, and sentinels armed with rifles and wearing the traditional sugar-loaf hat are standing on the roof-tops of Mulberry street ready to notify their comrades whenever a pedestrian ventures to enter a lonely pass between two beetling snow-heaps.

Whatever may be true as to brigandage, there are, doubtless, among the Neapolitan immigrants members of the Camorra [Italian Mafia-like organization based in Naples] who are ready to revive in this City the cheerful customs of that association. In the old days when the Camorra notified a respectable Neapolitan to pay a certain sum of money he promptly paid it, as the only way in which to avoid a knife thrust. The same system, if introduced here, would soon supersede our crude and native methods of blackmailing; and that it is practiced to a greater or less extent among the Italian immigrants themselves there is good reason to believe. After all, this is the true field for Neapolitan industry in this City; and as for brigandage pure and simple, the Italians, before engaging in it, should seriously ask themselves whether they can hope to succeed in such direct competition with that old and well-established class, the plumbers.

Anti-Italian Violence and Lynchings

Luciano J. Iorizzo and Salvatore Mondello

Thousands of southern Italian immigrants began entering the United States in the 1880s, just when the country was experiencing an economic downturn and a rise in nativist thinking. Nativists believed in preserving "traditional" American culture that, to them, meant northern European culture. The nativists viewed dark-skinned peasant farmers from southern Italy with suspicion and accused the new immigrants of being Mafia members devoted to a life of crime. More and more nativists began calling for restrictions on Italian immigration. Sporadic episodes of harassment and violence against Italians began to break out around the United States during this period. In this selection from their book *The Italian Americans*, Luciano J. Iorizzo and Salvatore Mondello describe the growing hostility toward Italian immigrants that led to horrendous violence in New Orleans in 1891. The city's chief of police, David C. Hennessy, was murdered, and many local residents became convinced that the Mafia was responsible. Since many Americans believed that all Italians belonged to the Mafia, nine Italian immigrants were tried for the crime. When none of the Italians were convicted, an angry mob gathered and broke into the parish prison and shot ten Italians to death in their cells. Another Italian who had only been wounded was dragged outside and lynched and shot many more times in front of a crowd. Mondello is a professor emeritus of American history at the Rochester Institute of Technology. Iorizzo teaches Italian American studies at the State University of New York at Oswego.

Luciano J. Iorizzo and Salvatore Mondello, *The Italian Americans*. Boston: Twayne Publishers, a division of G.K. Hall & Co., 1980. Copyright © 1980 by G.K. Hall & Co. All rights reserved. Reproduced by permission of the Gale Group.

During the 1880s the English-language press frequently noted that the South Italians were especially addicted to criminal behavior and that they lowered the standard of living in the United States. As early as 1884 the *Chicago Tribune* reported that some Italian bootblacks, in the traditional fashion of Italian outlaws, had attacked a policeman with wooden daggers. Four years later the *Tribune* observed that Chicago had to have a Mafia since it had many Sicilian immigrants.

In the *North American Review* for 1888 a more sweeping allegation was made by T.V. Powderly, who argued that those Europeans emigrating to America after the Civil War were for the most part semibarbarous. They received low wages, he commented, and spent most of their earnings on liquor. Other commentators were less vituperative in their language, but equally critical. One writer [W.M.F. Round] claiming that the Irish and Italians showed "a special tendency to crime," called for restricting their migration to America. . . .

Harassment of Italians

By the end of the eighties nativist diatribes were punctuated by sporadic public demands for repressive measures against the Italian immigrants; and law enforcement agents responded with such vengeance that diplomatic relations between Rome and Washington were severely strained. On March 4, 1888, the Buffalo superintendent of police ordered the arrest of virtually the entire Italian population of that city following the killing several days earlier of one Italian by another Italian immigrant. The dragnet led to the detention of 325 Italians, each of whom was searched for concealed weapons. The hasty police action of 1888 was an indicator of public hysteria rather than of the presence of numerous Italian criminals, for only two of the 325 suspects had weapons in their possession.

The terrorized Italian population of Buffalo was led to

appeal to Rome for protection against the Buffalo law enforcement authorities. The Italian consul general of New York and the Italian ambassador to Washington quickly registered protests against the arbitrary actions of the Buffalo police and demanded a full explanation. In his report to the governor of New York the Buffalo superintendent of police gave two major reasons for the mass arrests: the Italians and Poles of Buffalo made a regular practice of carrying concealed weapons; and the public had demanded vigorous police action to curtail crime among the city's foreign born residents.

As the strife-torn decade drew to a close Italian-American journalists began to see in the Italian vote the most effective means for containing the economic discrimination and violence which attended nativist prejudice. In 1890 *Il Progresso* urged its alien readers to become American citizens if they desired for themselves those privileges already possessed by German-Americans and Irish-Americans. "It is our vote that must count," the newspaper admonished.

This call to Italian-Americans to rally their forces and increase their political weight was scarcely farfetched; for invectives against the foreign born grew in intensity as the crises of the eighties merged with the deeper and more widespread agony of the nineties. The unremitting economic dislocation of the new decade, exacerbated by the depression of 1893–1897, caused countless Americans to see the foreign born as the harbingers of their misfortunes. In August, 1890, an alarmed journalist [Peri Andes] wrote that America was infected with foreign born anarchists, communists, and nihilists. These radicals, he believed, found their followers in the foreign born paupers, illiterate laborers, and criminals who had emigrated to the United States. A sense of duty to themselves and to the human race, he suggested, impelled Americans, who (in his opinion) were democracy's only hope, to suspend immigration.

Violence and Lynchings

Hysteria occasionally gave way to violence during the 1890s and Italians were counted among the victims. In Denver, Colorado, one Italian was lynched in 1893; of the nine Italian-American miners arrested on suspicion of murdering an American saloon keeper in Walsenburg, Colorado, two years later, one was found guilty while six others were executed by a mob. Two hundred Italians were driven out of Altoona, Pennsylvania, in 1894. Three Italians were lynched in Hahnville, Louisiana, in 1896, and five met a similar fate in Tallulah, Mississippi, three years later. With lynching parties led by respectable citizens and their violence condoned by the press, the United States came close to denying its humanitarian heritage. In its social implications the most significant lynching of Italians in America took place in New Orleans on March 14, 1891; for from that day until 1897 it seemed as though the entire Italian-American population was on trial in the United States.

The incident of 1891 was one grotesque consequence of the depressions, the political chaos, and the racial crisis which engulfed the South during the eighties and nineties. Poor white farmers and their spokesmen, frustrated by the inability of the ruling Southern conservatives to alleviate their plight, found new leadership in the Populist party and sought the cooperation of the equally depressed black population. The poor of both races surprised each other and amazed their political protagonists by their willingness to work together.

The conservatives, however, using fraud, intimidation, and terror against blacks and employing the shibboleth of white solidarity in their appeal to poor whites, succeeded in driving an irreparable wedge in the Populist alliance and thus regained their political power. The reconciliation of estranged white classes in the South was effected by sacrificing the black American, the approved sectional and national scapegoat.

The support which the Populists had found among the South Italians of New Orleans did not endear them to the ruling class of that city. Untrained in the bitter racial antagonisms of Southern politics, the Italians in New Orleans had joined the Populists in their protests against antiblack legislation. Moreover, the control exercised by Italian-American businessmen over Louisiana's fruit trade with Latin America deepened the resentment against the entire South Italian community in the city. In fact, one of the Italians executed in 1891 was a wealthy merchant and prominent in New Orleans political circles.

New Orleans Incident

In 1890 David C. Hennessy, the New Orleans chief of police, was murdered. The Italians were suspected of the killing, for Hennessy had acquired a favorable reputation in his popular investigations of criminal activities among the Sicilians of Decatur Street. Convinced that the Mafia had planned the execution, a "law and order" organization, the "Committee of Fifty," headed by a prominent white supremacist, was formed to find those *mafiosi* who were believed responsible for the shooting.

To the consternation of the vigilantes, on March 12, 1891, of the nine Italians tried for the crime, six were acquitted and a mistrial was declared for the other three. Two days later two outraged local politicians, assisted by the editor of the *New Delta*, led a mass rally before the statue of Henry Clay. Conspicuous for their presence were many of New Orleans' prominent citizens. One of the politicians, W.S. Parkerson, asked the multitude to fall in line, marched the group around the statue three times and then stated:

> When courts fail, the people must act. What protection
> or assurance of protection is there left as when the very

head of our Police Department, our Chief of Police, is assassinated in our very midst by the Mafia Society and his assassins are again turned loose on the community? Will every man here follow me and see the murder of Hennessy avenged? Are there men enough here to set aside the verdict of that infamous jury, every one of whom is a perjurer and a scoundrel.

Following this exhortation the mob made its way to the parish prison. Meeting no resistance from the sheriff and his deputies, the jail was entered and ten Italians were shot to death. It was decided that another Italian who had only been wounded was to be executed in the presence of those citizens who were waiting outside the jail and were anxious to witness a public hanging. The public sacrifice was reported by the New Orleans press and the story was reprinted in the *New York Times* on March 15:

> Polize, the crazy man, was locked up in a cell upstairs. The doors were flung open and one of the avengers, taking aim, shot him through the body. He was not killed outright and in order to satisfy the people on the outside, who were crazy to know what was going on within, he was dragged down the stairs and through the doorway by which the crowd had entered. A rope was provided and tied around his neck and the people pulled him up to the crossbars. Not satisfied that he was dead, a score of men took aim and poured a volley of shot into him, and for several hours the body was left dangling in the air.

Satisfied with the day's developments, the crowd shouted its approval of what had transpired, paraded back to the statue of Clay with Parkerson on the shoulders of several of the proud citizens of the city, and then dispersed.

The incident of 1891 marked a turning point in nativist thought, for it encouraged the conviction that the Sicilians had at last established in America their centuries-old criminal conspiracy, the Mafia, which now threatened to disrupt

American society. Since evidence of the presence of the Sicilian Mafia in America appeared by 1891 to be irrefutable, many newspaper editors and private citizens were unanimous in their defense of the New Orleans citizenry's firm resolve to crush the Sicilian criminal organization in its community.

CHAPTER 2

The Italians' New Life in America

COMING TO AMERICA

An Italian Girl's Testimony About the 1912 Lawrence Textile Strike

Camella Teoli

Italian immigrants settled in all regions of the United States in the late nineteenth and early twentieth centuries. The majority, however, made their homes in the large cities of the East where they worked as laborers in mines and in factories. Entire families went to work in New England's textile mills where they were forced to pay high prices for food and rent while wages stayed low and working hours were long. Laborers were even charged for their drinking water. Conditions in the mills were so bad that 36 percent of the workers died before the age of twenty-five.

In 1912 when the Massachusetts state legislature passed a statute reducing weekly work hours from fifty-six to fifty-four for women and children under eighteen, officials of the American Woolen Company in Lawrence reduced workers' pay. In protest, the workers walked out of the mills, initiating one of America's largest labor strikes. When thirty thousand workers speaking some fifty languages refused to return to work, the factories were forced to shut down. About seven thousand of the strikers were Italian immigrants. The militia was called, violence broke out, and martial law was declared. As the strike wore on, workers tried to send their starving children to homes elsewhere so that the children would at least be fed, but the police beat back the workers and their children at the train station.

Camella Teoli, testimony before the U.S. Congress, Washington, DC, March 1912.

This brutal treatment so disturbed the American public that a congressional hearing was called. The following selection is an extract of the testimony of one of the mill workers, fourteen-year-old Camella Teoli. She describes a horrendous injury she suffered while working in the mill and offers a simple explanation of why she went on strike: She was hungry and the mills did not pay a living wage. In the face of such bad publicity and with public sentiment against them, the mill owners conceded and offered the workers a 15 percent salary increase, time and a quarter for overtime hours (overtime was previously unpaid), and no reprisals for the strikers. The workers, whose slogan was "We want bread and roses, too," emerged victorious.

Chairman: Camella, how old are you?

   Miss Teoli: Fourteen years and eight months.

   Chairman: Fourteen years and eight months?

   Miss Teoli: Yes.

   Chairman: How many children are there in your family?

   Miss Teoli: Five.

   Chairman: Where do you work?

   Miss Teoli: In the woolen mill.

   Chairman: For the American Woolen Co.?

   Miss Teoli: Yes.

   Chairman: What sort of work do you do?

   Miss Teoli: Twisting.

   Chairman: You do twisting?[1]

   Miss Teoli: Yes.

   Chairman: How much do you get a week?

   Miss Teoli: $6.55.

   Chairman: What is the smallest pay?

   Miss Teoli: $2.64.

   Chairman: Do you have to pay anything for water?

   Miss Teoli: Yes.

---

1. working on a twister machine that twists strands into thicker yarn or rope

Chairman: How much?

Miss Teoli: 10 cents every two weeks.

Chairman: Do they hold back any of your pay?

Miss Teoli: No.

Chairman: Have they ever held back any?

Miss Teoli: One week's pay.

Chairman: They have held back one week's pay?

Miss Teoli: Yes. . . .

Work Injury

Chairman: Now, did you ever get hurt in the mill?

Miss Teoli: Yes.

Chairman: Can you tell the committee about that—how it happened and what it was?

Miss Teoli: Yes.

Chairman: Tell us about it now, in your own way.

Miss Teoli: Well, I used to go to school, and then a man came up to my house and asked my father why I didn't go to work, so my father says I don't know whether she is 13 or 14 years old. So, the man say you give me $4 and I will make the papers come from the old country saying you are 14. So, my father gave him the $4, and in one month came the papers that I was 14. I went to work, and about two weeks got hurt in my head.

Chairman: Now, how did you get hurt, and where were you hurt in the head; explain that to the committee?

Miss Teoli: I got hurt in Washington.

Chairman: In the Washington Mill?

Miss Teoli: Yes, sir.

Chairman: What part of your head?

Miss Teoli: My head.

Chairman: Well, how were you hurt?

Miss Teoli: The machine pulled the scalp off.

Chairman: The machine pulled your scalp off?

Miss Teoli: Yes, sir.

Chairman: How long ago was that?

Miss Teoli: A year ago, or about a year ago.

Chairman: Were you in the hospital after that?

Miss Teoli: I was in the hospital seven months.

Chairman: Seven months?

Miss Teoli: Yes.

Chairman: Did the company pay your bills while you were in the hospital?

Miss Teoli: Yes, sir.

Chairman: The company took care of you?

Miss Teoli: The company only paid my bills; they didn't give me anything else.

Chairman: They only paid your hospital bills; they did not give you any pay?

Miss Teoli: No, sir.

Chairman: But paid the doctors bills and hospital fees?

Miss Teoli: Yes, sir.

Mr. Lenroot: They did not pay your wages?

Miss Teoli: No, sir.

Chairman: Did they arrest your father for having sent you to work for 14?

Miss Teoli: Yes, sir.

Chairman: What did they do with him after they arrested him?

Miss Teoli: My father told this about the man he gave $4 to, and then they put him on again.

Chairman: Are you still being treated by the doctors for the scalp wound?

Miss Teoli: Yes, sir.

Chairman: How much longer do they tell you, you will have to be treated?

Miss Teoli: They don't know.

Chairman: They do not know?

Miss Teoli: No.

Chairman: Are you working now?

Miss Teoli: Yes, sir.

Chairman: How much are you getting?

Miss Teoli: $6.55. . . .

Chairman: How long did you go to school?

Miss Teoli: I left when I was in the sixth grade.

Chairman: You left when you were in the sixth grade?

Miss Teoli: Yes, sir.

Chairman: And you have been working ever since, except while you were in the hospital?

Miss Teoli: Yes, sir. . . .

The Mill Strike

Mr. Hardwick: Are you one of the strikers?

Miss Teoli: Yes, sir.

Mr. Hardwick: Did you agree to the strike before it was ordered; did they ask you anything about striking before you quit?

Miss Teoli: No.

Mr. Hardwick: But you joined them after they quit?

Miss Teoli: Yes.

Mr. Hardwick: Why did you do that?

Miss Teoli: Because I didn't get enough to eat at home.

The Trial of Sacco and Vanzetti

Eli C. Bortman

Nicola Sacco and Bartolomeo Vanzetti were two Italian immigrant anarchists who were convicted and executed in 1927 for committing two murders during a robbery in South Braintree, Massachusetts, in 1920. Many Americans in the early twentieth century viewed immigrant political radicals such as Sacco and Vanzetti as a threat to American society, especially after the Russian Revolution of 1917. The political radicals, however, saw themselves as activists in a mighty struggle to secure rights for workers and immigrants. Sacco and Vanzetti's trial was considered so unfair that considerable public sympathy developed for the two men, especially among many American liberals and intellectuals. Historians agree that the judge was prejudiced and that the trial was biased. Furthermore, many historians consider the conviction and execution of Sacco and Vanzetti as a form of legal lynching. On the other hand, some historians believe that while Vanzetti was surely innocent, they are not sure about Sacco. In 1977, Massachusetts governor Michael Dukakis declared that the executions had been unfair. In this selection from *History in Dispute*, Eli C. Bortman, an attorney and frequent contributor to books on American history, describes the prejudiced conditions of the trial and the evidence that was presented by the prosecution. Bortman is also a visiting professor at Babson University in Wellesley, Massachusetts.

Eli C. Bortman, "Sacco and Vanzetti," *History in Dispute, Volume 3: American Social and Political Movements, 1900–1945*, edited by Robert J. Allison. Farmington Hills, MI: St. James Press. All rights reserved. Reproduced by permission of the Gale Group.

On 24 December 1919 two armed robbers attempted to hold up a truck that was delivering a payroll to a factory in Bridgewater, Massachusetts. Several shots were fired, but the truck escaped. The robbers fled on foot to a waiting getaway car. Eyewitnesses described the gunmen as "dark-complexioned foreigners," one of whom had a mustache. An informant told police that the crime was the work of Italian anarchists living in the area. On 15 April 1920 two men shot and killed a payroll clerk and his guard as they walked on a busy street in South Braintree, Massachusetts. Two or three accomplices in a getaway car picked up the gunmen and the payroll boxes. As in the previous case, an eyewitness described one of the gunmen as a "short, swarthy, foreigner." Three weeks later, [Nicola] Sacco and [Bartolomeo] Vanzetti, both active in an anarchist group, were arrested, almost by accident. Once the police thought that Sacco and Vanzetti might be the Bridgewater holdup men and the Braintree killers, they convinced eyewitnesses to identify them. Vanzetti was charged with the Bridgewater attempt, quickly tried, and convicted. Immediately after this trial Sacco and Vanzetti were charged with the Braintree murders.

To understand why the trial and eventual execution of Sacco and Vanzetti were so controversial, one has to appreciate the political and social climate of the times. . . .

Unregulated Capitalism and Labor Unrest

The United States was in the laissez-faire phase of the industrial age in the early twentieth century. Capitalism was unfettered, and few laws protected labor. Factory conditions were terrible for employees; hours were long and wages were so low that workers seemed doomed to lives of poverty. Unions were not entitled to any legal protection—rather, they were considered illegal conspiracies. Factory owners could count on judicial injunctions to block organizers or stop strikes; owners often resorted to ordinary violence instead of waiting for legal proceedings. Efforts to organize critical industries had resulted in several large strikes around the country, often with violent endings, such as those involving iron miners in Minnesota; oil workers in Tulsa, Oklahoma; and textile workers in Lawrence, Massachusetts, to name a few. The industrial climate was particularly tense in New England, as labor unrest was starting to take its toll. The textile industry was drifting to the South and the shoe industry to the West, both areas with more-docile workers than New England, where labor agitators were considered public enemies.

In addition to labor problems, large numbers of immigrants had been arriving in New England for years. Native-born workers resented the influx of competitors for the factory jobs that already paid low wages. Crime, poverty, disease, life in overcrowded tenements, and separation from natives and other immigrant populations by strange languages and appearances produced constant social tension for immigrants.

World War I produced an explosive growth of patriotic fervor that fostered efforts to protect America from various perceived threats. Federal legislation enacted during the war (the Espionage Act, Sedition Act, and an amended Immigration Act) formed the basis for rooting out spies, radicals, slackers, anarchists, communists, and socialists. Anti-German ardor during the war became anti-Bolshevik fervor after the war. The mechanisms for discovering wartime spies were also used to attack the labor-union movement. The general public did not differentiate among anarchists, socialists, communists or labor organizers: all were deemed threats to U.S. national security. Government agencies and private vigilante groups mobilized to expose disloyalty of every type. The Immigration Act provided a new weapon—deportation—for the authorities to use against foreign-born advocates of anarchy.

Sacco and Vanzetti

These three themes of public opinion and official concern—labor unrest, xenophobia, and the Red Scare[1]—converged on Nicola Sacco and Bartolomeo Vanzetti. Sacco was born in Italy in 1891 and came to Boston in 1908. After working at a variety of unskilled jobs, he learned to operate a shoemaking machine and entered the ranks of skilled factory labor. He joined the social clubs and naturalization groups where politics and the workers' struggles were the usual topics of discussion. This activity led him to the labor movement, as well as to union and anarchist activities. He raised money to feed striking workers and to provide legal defense for union leaders. He organized picket lines and protest rallies. In May 1917, when the United States entered World War I, Sacco joined a group of Italians who went to Mexico to avoid the draft. He came back in 1918 and returned to his shoe-factory job.

Vanzetti was born in Italy in 1888 and immigrated to New York in 1908. He worked at several unskilled jobs, eventually settling in Plymouth, Massachusetts, where he loaded coils of rope at the shipping dock of a cordage factory. Vanzetti also joined the labor and anarchist circles, and he became a writer and speaker in behalf of these groups. In 1916, when the cordage-plant workers struck for higher wages, Vanzetti stepped into a leadership position. In 1917 he went with the same group as Sacco to Mexico, where the two men became close friends. Shortly after Vanzetti returned to Plymouth, he bought a fish peddler's cart and worked on his own. . . .

The trial for the Braintree robbery and murders began in May 1921, in Dedham, a suburb of Boston. Pretrial sensationalism labeled the defendants as "dangerous Reds."

1. A period of intense anticommunism in the United States. The widespread fear of communism led to aggressive investigation and sometimes persecution of people associated with Communist (or Socialist) ideology or political movements.

Local and state police were on hand in large numbers to prevent the defendants' associates from attempting a rescue. For six weeks the trial progressed, and the intensity of the press coverage never wavered. [Webster] Thayer, the same judge who had presided over Vanzetti's earlier trial,[2] had a year before made public his feelings about the anarchist movement and its writings. In a speech to a group of newly naturalized citizens, he said "How unfortunate that such [writing], so destructive in its character and so revolutionary in its tendencies should ever have reached the sacred shores of these United States." He showed his prejudice against the defendants throughout the trial. In his introductory remarks to the jury he praised the jurors for serving "in the spirit of supreme American loyalty." Whenever the prosecution attempted to inflame the jurors' patriotic fervor, Thayer indulged the effort.

The evidence against the two men can be grouped in three categories—eyewitness identification, the defendants' "consciousness of guilt," and ballistics. The judge's bias was evident throughout the trial. The prosecutor presented eleven eyewitnesses. Months earlier at pretrial hearings every one of these witnesses had said that the events were too quick and exciting for them to have made definite identifications. At the trial, however, a full year after the shooting, their opinions were firmly held—seven witnesses testified that they saw Sacco either before, during, or after the shooting. No one testified that Vanzetti was one of the gunmen. One witness said he had seen Vanzetti shortly before the crime—he claimed he saw a car with five foreigners in it and recognized Vanzetti as the man in the middle in the back seat. Two others, both railroad-crossing guards, testified that they had seen Vanzetti in the car after the shooting; one said Vanzetti was the driver, while the other,

2. Vanzetti was tried and convicted, perhaps unjustly, in 1920, for the Bridgewater robbery.

who saw the car at a different crossing, said Vanzetti was in the front passenger seat.

The second type of evidence was described by Thayer as "consciousness of guilt." Sacco and Vanzetti were arrested three weeks after the crime, when they went to borrow Boda's car. They lied to the police about why they were in Bridgewater that evening, made gestures (the police said) as if they were reaching for guns, and lied about the names of their comrades. Vanzetti was carrying a gun, he lied about when and from whom he had bought it. Both men lied about how long they had known each other. Of course, the two men were aware of the roundups of radicals, of the government's efforts to deport alien radicals, and of the recent death of Salsedo.[3] At the time of arrest they were on their way to hide incriminating literature. They had lied to the police to avoid incriminating themselves with respect to their anarchist activities and to avoid identifying their colleagues. The defense had to disclose this information in order to explain why they had lied. The prosecution pounced on the political subject matter in order to play to the jurors' prejudices. The judge allowed this prejudicial theme to be injected into the trial, saying that it bore upon the defendants' "consciousness of guilt."

The third category of the evidence was the guns Sacco and Vanzetti were carrying when they were arrested. Four bullets were removed from the body of the payroll guard. The science of ballistics was in its infancy at the time, and several experts agreed that they could not tell whether three of them had come from Sacco's weapon. One of the bullets presented at the trial, however, had the distinctive markings that allowed the experts to tie that bullet to the barrel of Sacco's gun. No one offered any explanation about why one bullet was so different from the other three.

3. Andrea Salsedo, who published radical literature in Italian, was arrested and died under mysterious circumstances while in custody awaiting deportation.

(Later, in the appeals after the trial, the defense presented evidence, to no avail, that the police had switched this bullet with the bullet actually removed from the dead guard's body.) Additional evidence was the prosecution's assertion that the gun Vanzetti had when he was arrested had belonged to one of the dead guards, taken from him at the time of the holdup. There was no documentary evidence, such as a serial number, connecting a gun the guard had purchased years earlier to the one Vanzetti had. Rather, the prosecution relied on witnesses' testimony about the type of gun they recalled the guard owning and a gunsmith's recollection of having repaired a similar gun for the guard a year earlier.

Prejudiced Atmosphere in the Court

The prejudicial atmosphere throughout the trial overcame whatever doubts the jurors might have had with respect to the evidence. The prosecutor used every opportunity to solicit the defendants' views on the economy, socialism, patriotism, and the recent war in order to play to the jurors' biases. Thayer allowed, and even participated in, this approach. For example, the prosecutor's first question to Vanzetti in the trial, when he began cross-examination, was "So you left Plymouth, Mr. Vanzetti, in May 1917 to dodge the draft, did you? While this country was at war, you ran away so you would not have to fight as a soldier?" Later, when the prosecutor asked Sacco several questions about his reason for going to Bridgewater the night he was arrested, Thayer interrupted with the question: "Is it your claim that the collection of the literature and the books and papers was done in the interest of the United States?"

The Guilty Verdict

The jury deliberated for five hours and returned verdicts of guilty of first-degree murder. News of the convictions was followed by protests and demonstrations across the country and abroad. A protest at the U.S. Embassy in Rome led to one hundred arrests. A bomb damaged the embassy in Paris; another bomb was intercepted in Lisbon. The State Department issued a summary of the case to help the foreign-service officers respond to the protests. Events abroad seemed to increase the domestic press's interest in the case.

The defense team filed a series of motions for a new trial. The law at the time provided that the judge at the original trial was the only person who could rule on these motions. These motions and his rulings are further proof of the miscarriage of justice. One motion asserted that one of the jurors had brought illegal exhibits in the jury room—some bullets similar to those presented as evidence—to help his fellow jurors learn about bullets. Two eyewitnesses confessed (after the trial was over) to having perjured themselves when they had identified Sacco; both claimed they had been coerced by the prosecution. The defense team learned after the trial that one witness was a notorious crook who was wanted for larceny and who was apparently allowed to avoid prosecution in return for his eyewitness account. In 1925 a man named Madeiros, on death row for another killing, confessed to the Braintree holdup; this man swore that Sacco and Vanzetti were not involved. The judge denied each of these motions.

The defense team's efforts to secure a new trial or a reversal on appeal received some moral support from the press and liberal academics. Several newspapers that had at first agreed with the jury's verdict and the trial judge's rulings changed their positions as additional facts came to light, and they published editorials favoring a new trial. The *Boston Herald* won a Pulitzer Prize for its 1926 editorial in which it explained why it now criticized the judge it had previously backed. Felix Frankfurter, then a professor at Harvard Law School, and later a U.S. Supreme Court Justice, published a lengthy article in *Atlantic Monthly* in which he analyzed the court record. He argued that the judge's bias throughout the trial demonstrated that Sacco and Vanzetti were not treated fairly. As was the case among many of the liberal academics, Frankfurter did not assert that Sacco and Vanzetti were necessarily innocent—his point was that a new trial was necessary to restore public confidence in the judicial system.

In 1926 the Massachusetts Supreme Judicial Court upheld Thayer's decisions, denying each motion for a new trial. Sacco and Vanzetti returned to face Thayer in April 1927 for sentencing. They had one last hope of avoiding the electric chair—a plea to Governor Alvin T. Fuller for commutation or clemency. The enormous and continuing public outcry prompted the governor to appoint a special blue-ribbon panel to review the case and advise him about commutation. Two college presidents and a retired judge interviewed many of the original witnesses and jurors over a period of about four weeks. Their report summarily dismissed all evidence that favored the defendants and seemed to accept all testimony against them. The panel decided that the jury was correct, and the governor accepted their report.

Another flurry of legal maneuvers followed—petitions in state and federal courts for a new trial, for a stay of execution, and appeals from the denials of motions, all the way to the U.S. Supreme Court, all in a matter of weeks, but to no avail. On 23 August 1927 Sacco and Vanzetti died in the electric chair in Charlestown, Massachusetts.

Fiorello La Guardia: Childhood Experiences and Political Beliefs

Fiorello La Guardia

By the first quarter of the twentieth century Italians had already begun the process of assimilation and integration into American civic life. One of the most prominent Italian Americans of this time was Fiorello La Guardia, who was born in New York in 1882 to Italian immigrant parents. La Guardia served in the U.S. Air Force during World War I and entered public life when he was elected as a Republican to the U.S. Congress in 1923. After serving for ten years, he was elected mayor of New York City in the middle of the Great Depression—an office he held until 1945. La Guardia was known as an honest and courageous liberal reformer who fought against political corruption and for the interests of the poor and working class. As mayor, he led the development of low-rent housing and public health services. Charismatic and beloved by New Yorkers, he was often called the Little Flower, a play on his first name. In this excerpt from his autobiography *The Making of an Insurgent*, La Guardia explains that his political beliefs and concern for the underdog grew from childhood experiences in Arizona, where La Guardia lived when his father served as a musician in the U.S. Army band. La Guardia saw Native American children forced to go without food, and army families cheated out of money because of the graft and corruption in the local government. He also describes his experiences of prejudice and his early observations of the struggles of immigrant laborers to survive—

Fiorello La Guardia, *The Making of an Insurgent: An Autobiography: 1882–1919.* Philadelphia: J.B. Lippincott, 1948.

all formative events that helped develop his crusading spirit as a congressman and mayor.

What I saw and heard and learned in my boyhood days in Arizona made lasting impressions on me. Many of the things on which I have such strong feelings—feelings which some of my opponents have regarded as unreasonable obsessions—were first impressed on my mind during those early days, and the knowledge I acquired then never left me. On some of those things I believe I am so right in my attitude that I remain uncompromising.

Professional Politicians

For instance, there is the professional politician. Though I have been in politics for well over forty years, I loathe the professional politician. I have never been a regular. I have fought political machines and party politics at every opportunity. This attitude had its origin in the loudly dressed, slick and sly Indian agents, political appointees, I saw come into Arizona. The first time I ever heard the word politician was at Fort Huachuca, when I was still a small child. The word was applied to those Indian agents. I learned afterwards that they got the jobs because they were small-fry ward heelers. I saw hungry Indians, and the little Indian kids watched us while we munched a Kansas apple or ate a cookie Mother baked. I knew, even as a child, that the government in Washington provided food for all those Indians, but that the "politicians" sold the rations to miners and even to general stores, robbing the Indians of the food the government provided for them. That was my first contact with "politicians."

I had my first experience with a lobby when I was about twelve. My father received a letter from someone in Washington stating that the pay of band leaders could be increased to $100 a month. The pay was then $60 a month. The letter also stated that band leaders could become commissioned officers. I can see the gleam in Dad's eye to this day as he fancied himself adorned with shoulder straps. It all seemed so easy: just sign the agreement to pay one month's salary when the bill became the law, and no further obligation except to send $50 for necessary expenses.

Even as a kid I could not understand this. Why the expenses? There were hints in the letter that it was necessary to see certain Representatives and Senators, and that there were disbursements to be met. It was rather crude. But this technique of the 'nineties didn't differ so much from the technique of our own 'forties. I don't know why, but I felt instinctively that it was wrong. And Mother was on my side. I figured it out that if the men in the various regiments at our post sent in this money, it would amount to $2,250. That was a lot of money in those days. "It's a fake, a swindle," I shouted, and when I ran out of adjectives in denouncing the scheme to my father, I resorted to what to me has always been the most odious thing you could say about people: "They're a bunch of politicians." Father, a musician, who never bothered with politics, was soon talked out of joining the plan. The band leaders of the Army are still waiting for those shoulder straps some of them sent their money to get.

Gamblers

My Arizona days made a lasting impression on me of the "tinhorn" and his ways. Professional gamblers in the West were known as "tinhorns." To me they have been "tinhorns" ever since. But there is one thing that could be said about the professional gambler of over a half century ago in the West: if he was alive, it was a fair assumption that he had not been caught gypping. Gamblers and saloonkeepers were an important part of pioneer Western life, but they were never a reputable part of the community. I remember very well how it used to be said that a gambler or a saloonkeeper could not join the Masons or the Elks. Gamblers were tolerated and patronized but not accepted. If a "tinhorn" in the West was caught cheating, he would never play another game—and there was no coroner's inquest. When I became Mayor of New York, I did my best to make life unpleasant for "tinhorns." They did not have to worry about being shot when caught red-handed, but they were made to fear the law.

My first attempt at applied mathematics—I must have been fourteen or fifteen then—was to figure out the percentage against the player in a crap game, a faro game and what was then called "policy," now known as "the numbers" and other fancy names as well as the old name "policy." Nearly every saloon in Prescott, Arizona, had its gambling department, mainly crap, faro and some Chinese game. There was, of course, a good deal of poker played— not under professional auspices. These games must have been exciting, according to the stories we kids would hear: the guns were laid on the table at easy reach, and of course the games were on the level.

Then "policy" came to town. I remember Mother telling me that it was the same as Lotto, which was sponsored in her native Trieste by the city or the state. Mother would play a ten-cent policy slip almost every week. If she had an exceptional dream, she would risk a quarter. She never won. No one else I knew ever won. The game did not last very long in Prescott and folded up after a few months. I figured it out then as nothing but petty larceny from the pockets of the poor, and showed my mother how she couldn't win.

I was astounded when I finally returned to New York to live in 1908 to find the great influence there of professional gamblers, numbers monarchs, and big "bookies," among others, with close political and judicial connections. They also had many, many friends among the press. I do not mean the reporters. It is easy for this scum of society, these economic vermin, to make friends when they are able to take bets and pay cash if the influential one "happens" to win, and to give unlimited credit if Mr. Big Shot happens to lose. They are no good. They never were any good in Prescott, or New York, and they never will be any good anywhere.

Immigrant Labor

Another early impression that made its mark on my mind was gained from watching the railroad being built between Ashfork, Prescott and Phoenix. There was no machinery used then. It was all manpower and draft animals. The laborers were all immigrants, mostly Mexicans and Italians. If a laborer was injured, he lost his job. If he was killed, no one was notified, because there was no record of his name, address or family. He just had a number. As construction moved on, it left in its wake the injured, the jobless, the stranded victims. Even as a young boy, this struck me as all wrong, and I thought about it a great deal. The more I thought about it, the less able was I to make sense out of that kind of situation. Years later, when I studied law, I learned about such things as "assumed risk," "the fellow servant rule," "contributory negligence," and other similar principles of law, all for the benefit of the employer. I still thought they were all wrong, and later, as a legislator, I did what little I could to have these antiquated eighteenth century rules of law changed. None of them are in use today. Employers' liability, workmen's compensation laws for injury, safeguards against accidents, sanitary and safety laws in factories and for other jobs, unemployment insurance have taken their place. It was this early glimpse of the condition of working people, of their exploitation and their utter lack of protection under the law, which prompted me to take an interest on their side in society. I hope I have made a contribution to progress in this respect.

I remember when the troops were called out to guard the property of the Atlantic & Pacific Railroad during the great Pullman strike of 1894. I was twelve years old then, and it was the first strike I ever knew. I was deeply interested. The whole thing had started with a small group of workers in the bedding department of the Pullman Company, and it spread until it became a general railroad strike throughout the entire country. Even then, as a boy, it occurred to me that surely there should be some way of settling labor disputes of this kind, and that the law should afford equal protection to both sides. I recognized the necessity for President Cleveland's order that there should be no interference with transportation of the United States mail. But I did not quite understand why it was unlawful for employees to inform other employees of grievances, or why they should be kept away from one another by a court mandate, enforced by bayonets of United States soldiers. These memories were very helpful. It was nearly a lifetime later, as a member of Congress, that I had the opportunity of taking part in preparing the Railways Labor Act and in the passage of the Norris-La Guardia Anti-injunction Act. The job is not yet completed. Satisfactory machinery for equitable and just settlement of labor disputes is still required. I do hope some day to see that job completed.

Racism and the Organ-Grinder

I also got my first glimpse of racial feeling born of ignorance, out there in Arizona. I must have been about ten when a street organ-grinder with a monkey blew into town. He, and particularly the monkey, attracted a great deal of attention. I can still hear the cries of the kids: "A dago with a monkey! Hey, Fiorello, you're a dago too. Where's your monkey?" It hurt. And what made it worse, along came Dad, and he started to chatter Neapolitan with the organ-grinder. He hadn't spoken Italian in many years, and he seemed to enjoy it. Perhaps, too, he considered the organ-grinder a fellow musician. At any rate, he promptly invited him to our house for a macaroni dinner. The kids taunted me for a long time after that. I couldn't understand it. What difference was there between us? Some of their families hadn't been in the country any longer than mine.

I have heard Gilbert and Sullivan's *Pinafore* [light opera] in almost every language, in many countries; and in the rendition of the song, "For He Is an Englishman," the traditional gesture mimicking the organ-grinder and the word "Eyetalian" always annoyed me.

Early in my first administration as Mayor, a traffic report by the Police Department showed that among the obstacles to free traffic was the nuisance of the street organ-grinder. It was with a great deal of gusto that I banned the organ-grinder from the streets of the City of New York. It caused some resentment among those who were sentimental about organ-grinders. One woman came up to me at a social function and berated me mildly for depriving her of her favorite organ-grinder. "Where do you live?" I asked. "Park Avenue," she said. "What floor?" "The fourteenth," she answered.

In addition to the fact that I never did like organ-grinders ever since my days of ridicule in Prescott when that one organ-grinder came to town, I felt that they made our traffic problem in New York more difficult. I was accused by some New Yorkers who liked them of having no sentimental feelings about organ-grinders, of having no soul, of oppressing the poor, of neglecting more important things to deprive old residents and young children of their pleasure. Some of my correspondents were genial and some were angry. Cornelia Otis Skinner, Beatrice Kauffman, Viola Irene Cooper were among the literary defenders of the hurdy-gurdy. Petitions were got up urging me to rescind the order. My answer to my critics was that there had been a time when the hurdy-gurdy was the only means of bringing music to many people. That was also the time before automobiles filled our streets. With the advent of the phonograph and the radio that time had passed. Free public concerts in parks, libraries, museums and other public places had given ample opportunity to hear music. But, more important, traffic conditions had changed. Children were endangered by trucks and other automobiles when they gathered in the middle of streets to hear and watch the organ-grinders. Also, the simple, sentimental hurdy-gurdy man had become a victim of a racket. My sentimental correspondents did not realize that the Italians' instruments were rented to them by *padrones* [labor contractors] at exorbitant fees. Their licenses from the city were in reality licenses to beg. About a year before I banned the organ-grinders, I had terminated the contracts with musicians on city ferry boats on the grounds that these were merely licenses to beg issued by the city. Despite these reasons, which I gave to my correspondents in answer to their protests, the defenders of the hurdy-gurdy men kept on writing to me for over a year, and some of them warned me that they wouldn't vote again for a man without a soul.

Italian Americans and Organized Crime

Richard D. Alba

The Mafia was an organization based in western Sicily in the nineteenth century whose members depended upon personal relations, cooperation with corrupt local officials, and violent criminal behavior to achieve their goals. Most of the members were linked by family ties. During the years of massive Italian immigration to the United States in the late nineteenth and early twentieth centuries, some Mafiosi immigrated to the United States, but they were unable to reestablish the Mafia in America because the organization was too dependent upon the social relations of western Sicily to be transferred to another location. Instead, Mafiosi immigrants joined forces with disaffected young Italian immigrant men to establish criminal gangs in America that were known as the Black Hand. These gangs extorted money under threat of violence primarily from honest Italian immigrants. Despite the fact that the Sicilian Mafia was not a factor in American crime, stories about the Mafia entered the American public imagination during this period, and many Americans began to believe that all Italian immigrants were members of the Mafia.

During the 1920s, Mafiosi immigrated to America because they were fleeing the fascist government of Benito Mussolini in Italy. The immigrant Mafiosi joined forces with American criminal groups to participate in the illegal production and distribution of alcoholic beverages during Prohibition. After Prohibition was overturned, crime groups began to organize on a national scale and became entirely Americanized. Native-born Americans from vari-

Richard D. Alba, *Italian Americans: Into the Twilight of Ethnicity*. Englewood Cliffs, NJ: Prentice-Hall, Inc., 1985, pp. 95–99. Copyright © 1985 by Prentice-Hall, Inc. All rights reserved. Reproduced by permission of Prentice-Hall, a division of Simon & Schuster, Upper Saddle River, NJ.

ous ethnic groups, including Italians, took control of organized crime, and the old immigrants, including the Mafiosi, were squeezed out. In this selection from his book *Italian Americans: Into the Twilight of Ethnicity*, Richard D. Alba describes the new generation of thoroughly Americanized gangsters that formed "crime families"—"families" in name only because members were usually not related by blood or marriage. Italian American crime families cooperated with criminals from other ethnic groups, especially Jewish gangsters, and the families began to include gambling and other activities in the scope of their criminal endeavors. Despite the fact that organized crime was multiethnic, and limited to a small percentage of the Italian American population, the American public continued to associate all Italian Americans with criminal activity, and in particular, with the Mafia. Alba is a professor of sociology at the State University of New York at Albany.

Organized crime can be usefully thought of
can institution, a sector of the economy pro
goods and services and serving as a channel f
bility. It is, to be sure, a stigmatized institutio
ticipants are branded with the mark of unr
and whose proferred opportunities for powe
entail great risk, including the possible loss
For these reasons, it attracts chiefly the mem
standing ethnic groups. Their ethnic backgrounds are a
disadvantage added to the usual difficulty of achieving
more than modest mobility through legitimate routes; and
in the event they lack the appetite to take the hard road to
conventional success or are unwilling to settle for a pedestrian existence, they may perceive that the opportunities
of illicit enterprise outweigh its risks. Members of established ethnic groups, having more routine access to opportunities for decent jobs, are rarely tempted into organized crime careers.

It follows as a corollary that the forms that crime takes are constrained by a group's position in the larger society; and as this position changes, so does the character of its members' participation in crime. Hence, the large-scale mobility and acculturation of Italian Americans in the period 1930–70 was accompanied by parallel changes in Italian-American organized crime. The crucial ones were a completion of the breakout from the ethnic enclave into the wider society, and a consolidation of Italian criminal groups into crime "families," loosely linked in a national network.

Americanization of the Mobs

One important step was the "Americanization of the mobs," the replacement of Old World–style leaders by younger men who had grown up in America and were familiar with American ways. Americanization did not happen everywhere at once; its timing and sequence varied from one city to another. In Chicago, Americanization occurred before 1930, under the leadership of John Torrio and then Al Capone. In New York, the same process occurred in the early 1930s, when Lucky Luciano choreographed the elimination of two Old World–style capos (heads). Among the younger men, mostly born in Italy but reared in the United States, who rose in the aftermath of these killings were Luciano, Frank Costello, Albert Anastasia, and Vito Genovese. Their names were to dominate the public's perception of Italian-American organized crime in the ensuing decades.

The Americanization of the mobs was important for several reasons. One concerned the linkage among criminals, police, and politicians necessary for illicit enterprise to prosper. When crime is dominated by unacculturated men, their unease in an American environment makes the linkage fragile. Acculturated criminals move easily in the world outside the ghetto. The presence is more invisible and hence they are able to associate more freely with politicians and other men wielding legitimate power. Among Italian-American gangsters, Frank Costello, a gambling kingpin of the 1930s, 40s, and 50s, is perhaps the supreme example of this ease of movement in the legitimate world. His biographer [Leonard Katz], interviewing his many legitimate friends, who of course knew of his criminal career, found that they nonetheless viewed him as a "prince of a fellow."

Multiethnic Criminals

In addition, Americanized Italian gangsters were able to cooperate with criminals of other ethnic backgrounds. As a result, starting in the 1930s, the Wild West atmosphere of Prohibition was brought to an end. Violence continued, to be sure, but principally as a means of working out succession in leadership positions and of eliminating individuals who had trespassed against powerful figures, and not as a feature of a war of all against all. The most notable examples of cooperation occurred with Jewish gangsters in Northern big cities, New York, Chicago, Cleveland, and Detroit, and with national repercussions. Eastern European Jews had immigrated to the United States at the same time as southern Italians and also found many legitimate avenues of mobility closed off. Jewish gangsters therefore formed an important component of the "rackets" in many cities with large Jewish populations. In these, located in the industrial heartland of the East and Midwest, Jewish and Italian gangsters—including Meyer Lansky, Bugsy Siegel, Lepke Buchalter, Lucky Luciano, Frank Costello, and Albert Anastasia—linked up in the 1930s to form a powerful syndicate known to its insiders as "the combination" and later to the public as "Murder, Inc." The combination eliminated many of the independents and smaller groups that had survived Prohibition mayhem, and it rationalized control over the rackets, allowing crime bosses to work in their territories without constant competition from others. It was regionally based, and hence it did not truly control American organized crime. Independent criminal groups continued to exist outside the region it dominated. Nonetheless, the combination could project itself on a national and even an international scale, as is shown by its activities in Las Vegas, which it helped to establish, and in Havana.

Ethnically based Italian-American criminal organizations also appear to have become consolidated during the 1930s, entering a long period of stability in which the organizational forms and even the personnel occupying them remained relatively constant. Italian-American organizations existed alongside the multiethnic framework of the combination (their collective name, "Cosa Nostra," literally "Our Thing," perhaps signified their need to have something separate). The basic organizational unit, the crime "family," is of unclear origins. It does not coincide with Mezzogiorno [refers to southern Italy] prototypes, and it is not discernible in the crime of the early period of settlement. It represents an adaptation to American circumstances that appears to have become crystallized during Luciano's ascendancy. By the 1930s, the organizational form could be described in a way that more or less applied to Italian crime families throughout the country (though it should be noted, details varied from place to place). A family was headed by a *capo* or boss, aided by one or more underbosses. Underneath the level of leadership, "soldiers" were organized in small units called "regimes" or "decine" (which translates as "groups of ten"); each such unit had a head, a *caporegime* or *capodecina*. The men at the very bottom were criminal entrepreneurs, responsible for developing their own enterprises and providing those above them with a cut of the action.

Not only did the form crystallize, but so did the actual crime families. The five New York crime families that exist today existed in the early 1930s, and the same continuity occurs in other American cities. Moreover, since that time, the twenty-four Italian-American crime families in the country have been loosely linked through the mechanism of "the Commission," a small group of leaders who meet to discuss general problems and resolve jurisdictional disputes. Popular literature on the Mafia to the contrary, however, the Commission does not appear to direct Italian organized crime; crime families are essentially independent units.

Organized Crime After Prohibition

One other consequence of the Americanization of the mobs was essential. The acculturation of Italian-American crime bosses and their cooperation with non-Italian gangsters eased the transition from Prohibition. Prohibition officially came to an end in 1933, with the ratification of the Twenty-First Amendment; and as America became legally "wet" again, an important source of profits for organized crime dried up and a search for new sources began. Interest in gambling was renewed. In New York, Italians followed Dutch Schultz into the numbers racket in Harlem, taking over after his murder in 1935 the operations he had grabbed from Black numbers bankers. Italians and others created bookmaking enterprises, allowing bettors to gamble on horse and dog racing, and established illegal casinos to cater further to the gambling trade. The profits from gambling in turn fed loan-sharking operations, for which gamblers served as important customers. Also, perhaps following the model of Lepke Buchalter, who used the conflict between businessmen and labor unions as an entree into the garment industry and other trades, Italians burrowed into labor racketeering. To a large extent, the industries in which they established themselves were ones where Italian Americans formed a critical part of the labor force, such as New York's Fulton Fish Market and the East Coast docks. But this was not always the case. For a time in the 1930s, Italian and Jewish gangsters succeeded in controlling a motion picture and theater union, using it as a base to extort money from movie studios and theater owners.

In the decades following the 1930s, Italian Americans continued their rise to power and prominence in organized crime, and by the 1950s, they were gaining ascendancy over Jewish gangsters, whose influence was ebbing. Jewish participation in crime was essentially a one-generation phenomenon, and Jewish strength was not renewed by a continuing flow of young Jewish men into careers of crime. Hence, as Jewish gangsters departed from the underworld by death or retirement, they were not replaced. Buchalter died in the electric chair in 1944; Bugsy Siegel was murdered in 1947, apparently because he was blamed for what at the time seemed to be the failure of Las Vegas. The Jewish figures who remained, such as Meyer Lansky, moved away from the front lines of crime. As individuals, some remained very powerful, but their numbers became fewer and fewer. By the 1960s, Italian-American crime families had achieved a monopoly position over a number of spheres in many American cities.

Association of Italians with Crime

It was in the same decade that Italians came, as well, to dominate public attention to organized crime. Racketeers had received intermittent attention in the 1940s and 50s, but a new phase of public concern about organized crime was inaugurated by the spectacular revelations of Joseph Valachi, a soldier in a New York City crime family. Valachi testified about a secret society he called "Cosa Nostra" and focused the public eye squarely on Italian-American organized crime. His testimony helped give birth to a new perception of organized crime, namely, that it was the same as the "Mafia" and "Cosa Nostra."

This perception spurred a reinterpretation of American organized crime, in which a historically specific ethnic form was taken as the key to all organized crime in America. Accordingly, American crime history was revised to focus almost entirely on events among the Italians; only Prohibition remained a significant exception. Thereby, the revision, which purported to trace step by step the development of American organized crime from its antecedents in Sicily and southern Italy, suggested implicitly that organized crime in America was the product of an alien cultural ethos brought by southern Italian immigrants.

It took a while for the basic character of this new perspective on crime to become clear, but subsequent research has uncovered the extent to which it distorts basic facts about crime in America. In the revised history, inconvenient events faded into the background, while others that had previously seemed unimportant were elevated to prominence and given new twists of interpretation. A revealing example concerns the so-called Purge of the Greasers, alleged to be the pivotal event in the Americanization of the Mafia. According to the revised history, Americanization was accomplished in a wave of violence in a 24-hour period (September 11, 1931), when scores of old-time Mafiosi were murdered throughout the country at the direction of Lucky Luciano. The story of "Purge Day," as it came to be called, was based in substantial part on Valachi's account, and it bolstered the image of a unified, nationwide conspiracy, capable of acting on a national scale according to a single plan. However attractive it was from the new perspective, the story is almost certainly not true. Two investigators acting independently of each other, Humbert Nelli and Alan Block, have searched newspapers and records in many American cities in an attempt to verify the murderous score. Their researches have uncovered only a very few murders that might be connected with one another, almost all in the New York–New Jersey area. The notable one, known about long before the account of "Purge Day" came to public attention, was that of Salvatore Maranzano, an important crime figure, and insofar as there is any truth to the notion of a "purge of the greasers," it appears to have been an event connected to realignments in New York City's gangland.

Nonetheless, the public attention devoted to Italians in crime during the 1960s appeared to cast a shadow of ambiguity over the gains made by Italian Americans after World War II. Many Americans with Italian names felt stung by the new interpretation, which implied that the Italian-American cultural heritage was tainted with criminality, and by the vulgar popularizations of the purported story of the Mafia, which magnified the phenomenon, attributing to it a mythological aura. Some Italian Americans attempted to defend their group by denying altogether the existence of Italian-American organized crime, managing to damage their own credibility and subject Italians to ridicule, without denting the mythology. The ambiguity enveloping the status of Italian Americans seemed cemented in place by the events of Italian-American Unity Day, June 26, 1971, when thousands gathered in New York City to celebrate Italian pride. During the ceremonies, Joseph Colombo, founder of the Italian-American Civil Rights League and alleged to be a crime figure, was shot; according to the police, his shooting resulted from gangland disagreements.

An Italian American Social Worker Helps Immigrants

Angela Carlozzi-Rossi

Angela Carlozzi-Rossi was a first-generation Italian American who departed from the traditional role of immigrant Italian women by going to college and becoming a social worker. In 1934 she became the executive director of the Italian Welfare League, assisting Italian immigrants who had problems properly documenting their legal immigration status. Her ability to speak both English and Italian made her effective in working with the immigrants. During World War II she was able to help people who had been interned at the immigration center at Ellis Island, New York, as she describes in the next selection. Carlozzi-Rossi's account of her work with immigrants is part of a collection of immigrants' stories edited by Salvatore J. LaGumina, entitled *The Immigrants Speak: Italian Americans Tell Their Story.* LaGumina, a history professor at Nassau Community College in New York, is a founder of the American Italian Historical Association.

Much of my work in the early years of the [Italian Welfare] League was involved with assisting Italian immigrants who had incurred the official displeasure of the Immigration Office. These were the post-1924 years in which all the new immigrants had to be in possession of a document showing they had come in legally. Unaware that it was still

Angela Carlozzi-Rossi, "Angela Carlozzi-Rossi," *The Immigrants Speak: Italian Americans Tell Their Story,* edited by Salvatore J. LaGumina. New York: The Center for Migration Studies, 1979. Copyright © 1979 by The Center for Migration Studies. All rights reserved. Reproduced by permission.

possible to enter the country legally, these people resorted to illegal entry and then found it necessary to legitimatize their status or face deportation regardless of whether they had wives and children. The head of the Immigration Office at Ellis Island asked us if we would do something about these people, to help them straighten out their status prior to deportation. The authorities were anxious to have the situation corrected because they did not know what to do with the families that would be left after the husbands were deported. Thus, we now started working with the wives and children who, in many instances, were *bona fide* United States citizens and could not be deported with the illegal aliens. We tried to help in whatever way we could by filling out the necessary forms and by obtaining correct documents and the like for approval by the Immigration Office. If these prospective deportees could not be helped the frequent result was broken families. These were the years of the depression and, without the breadwinner at home, it was very difficult for the rest of the family. The wives often could not get work so we tried to assist. Since we were bilingual it was easy for us to help out families who did not speak English and complete the necessary forms for assistance. . . .

Helping Italians on Ellis Island

To get to Ellis Island you had to go by a ferry which came only once every hour. On my very first day I missed the boat. There were other people on Ellis Island who had been incarcerated there and needed clothing, shaving material, toothpaste and other little necessities of this sort. The money to pay for these supplies came largely from our organization while the food was supplied by the government. Until the immigrants became accustomed to this food more was thrown out than was eaten.

I was not so horribly impressed when I first went to

work on the Island because I had previously worked in a settlement house with similar types of people. In addition, I was anxious to help the Italians incarcerated there. My anxiety increased, however, when I learned that many of them being held there were victims of an overzealous official who had accidently misled them into giving wrong answers, or who was too punctilious about rules. During the war we had thousands of people on the Island. After December 7, 1941, the FBI rounded up Italians, Germans and Japanese and brought them to Ellis Island where they

After navigating an arduous processing system, most Italian immigrants were allowed to enter the United States.

slept in great dorms with double beds. For the most part, they were separated according to nationality. There was an interesting case of an immigrant who swept the dorm. He had lost his alien registration card and had come to the Island to report it six months earlier. Upon informing the authorities, he was told to wait until they could get around to him. Meanwhile, six months had passed. I went to the head of the Immigration Service and asked him if he ever checked his cases and I proceeded to tell him about the sweeper. The sweeper was then released and I put him into contact with his relatives who met him in Manhattan. Ironically, he had proved his loyalty to his adopted land by picking up empty cigarette packs and taking out the lead wrappings used then, and packing them into a sizeable ball. When I asked him what he was doing it he said, "I am working for the war effort". I went back to the immigration inspector and told him that if they had a better American on the Island they would have to show him to us.

We had many similar cases. My most memorable one is a story about this girl whose mother, a United States citizen living in Italy, had sent her daughter to the United States to live with relatives. These relatives, who lived in Binghamton, New York, did not want her and notified us of their decision. As it happened, she had a paraplegic cousin who agreed to take her, assuring me that he and his wife did want her and could take care of her. He told me to call the Bulova Watch Company for his reference. I told the girl she could live with her cousin, but that if she returned to Italy she could not stay there for more than a year. Eventually, she went back to Italy for a visit and I arranged for her to have a good place on the ship with good people. Less than a year afterward, I heard through the grapevine that she was back. Seeking her out I found that she had married a cousin in Italy whom she could call into the United States. Some months later she informed me that she had been a second prize winner on the Irish Sweepstakes, winning $56,000, of which she never sent one cent to the League. I was disappointed in this because we had done so much for her. Without us she would have been left stranded on the street.

War Brides

At the end of World War II there were a number of Italian war brides who came to Ellis Island and the Italian Welfare League interpreted for them and informed them of the requirements for lawful admission to the United States. For example, they would have to have $500 to assure the American government that, in case the young man refused to marry the Italian girl, she would have enough fare to return to Italy. A number of human interest stories emerged from this experience: some happy, some sad and some humane. I remember one little young lady who came to meet her boyfriend to get married, only to find out that he had married someone else. In the meantime, the boy's uncle came to see the girl every two weeks while she was waiting for the necessary paper work to return to Italy. Well, one day I was on a ship which had just arrived and was assisting in the interpreting, when I heard "Signora, Signora", and sure enough this girl, Marta, ran to me and told me that she had married the uncle and was now entering on a visa as the wife of an American citizen.

I also remember meeting one Italian girl on Ellis Island who was crying because her boyfriend had not come to meet her. All was not lost, however, because she had met a Japanese man and was going to marry him. She had been kept on the Island for some time during which she attempted suicide merely because she wanted to get off the Island. I told her she should not attempt that again because she would be sent back to Italy thereby extracting a promise that she would behave. In the meantime her Japanese boyfriend came with plenty of money to cover her bond. She married him and went to live with him in Hawaii. . . .

Assisting Immigrants and Internees

We had an unemployment service where we searched out Italian employers and referred our cases to them. Most of these employed artisans and manual laborers. We did not have to do anything in the construction trade since most of them had relatives, or *paesani* [countrymen] to get them into the trade. Even today [1979] many Italian immigrants are in construction. I also worked with an assistant of the unionist, Luigi Antonini, to place workers in the garment trade.

When World War II came, all the Italian sailors from the Italian ships in American ports were also shipped to Ellis Island. It was Roosevelt's idea to gather these sailors, even to the extent of going to South American countries and taking Italian sailors from Italian ships docked there, and bring them to the United States. He claimed they had to be interned because they were sabotaging ships. This was not so at all. I was very outspoken about this and probably jeopardized myself. In fact, my husband wondered aloud how I was never arrested. I rebuked American officials at Ellis Island in behalf of these Italian sailors saying that whatever they did to American ships was done in response to orders. They were, after all, Italians. There were hundreds of them on Ellis Island sleeping in double beds in a large room on the Island. Interned there were also a great many German people even women who had been placed there by the FBI. The FBI was very vigilant at that time. The Japanese were of course put into internment camps which I thought was bad because they were American citizens and not Japanese. I did not hesitate to tell the authorities that we were doing something wrong in this regard. The Italian sailors held on Ellis Island were not American citizens. Interestingly, a few of them were sent to Texas, where state authorities did not know what to do with them. Texas had no internment camps so they were kept in prisons until 10:00 at night when they were let out and allowed to cook for everybody there. . . .

A number of internees were released after investigation proved there were no grounds on which to hold them. I remember one time when I was instrumental in gaining the release of a large number of men who were to be released in their own recognizance after they posted $500 bonds. I informed them that they would not have to put up the money since they would be released anyway. This was part of my work as the official representative of the Italian Welfare League on Ellis Island. It was my responsibility to look after the legitimate interest of the Italian immigrants and aliens and I was conversant with the whole operation on Ellis Island. I also used to go to Washington once a month on cases to appear before the Board of Immigration Appeals. I had my license to practice before the Board in 1944. The Board members would listen carefully to my arguments on each case and then would tell me that they would inform me of their decision. Only one of my cases was deported in all of the 18 years I was there and this person was deported largely because I did not know the ropes when I first began. After that, however, I became much more familiar with the practices and legal traps. My work was a tremendous sense of satisfaction to me. If I had the strength I would go back to it today. Of course, it is entirely different today than it was in those years, but I would go back because it was a source of wonderful satisfaction to me. I was sometimes sworn at and, many things were said about me, but a simple "Thank you," wiped out everything else.

Escaping Italian Fascism

Riccardo Massoni

When Fascists led by Benito Mussolini took over the Italian government in the 1930s, many Italian Americans supported them because the Fascists were anti-Communists and promised to clean up criminal organizations such as the Mafia. Eventually Italian Americans came to realize that Mussolini was a dictator who ruled through his gangs of thugs known as Black Shirts. In the next selection Riccardo Massoni describes how his father in Italy was brutally attacked by the Fascists for refusing to join the party. Massoni and his family fled to Paris, and ultimately Massoni and his cousin immigrated to America. Massoni eloquently describes his struggle in America to make a living, to learn English, and to continue his education. His account is part of a collection of stories by immigrants in Joan Morrison and Charlotte Fox Zabusky's book *American Mosaic: The Immigrant Experience in the Words of Those Who Lived It*. Morrison is a freelance writer and adjunct professor at the New School for Social Research in New York. Zabusky supervises the Regional Immigration Assistance Center in Pittsburgh, Pennsylvania.

My father was a well-known anti-Fascist lawyer in Italy before the war. When I was a young boy, about six or seven years old, I remember him coming home once, all beaten up, with black and blue marks all over his head. The local Black Shirts [Fascist paramilitary gangs], they knew my father. At that time, Leghorn was only maybe a city of a hundred and twenty thousand people. In a city of that

Riccardo Massoni, "Riccardo Massoni," *American Mosaic: The Immigrant Experience in the Words of Those Who Lived It*, edited by Joan Morrison and Charlotte Fox Zabusky. New York: E.P. Dutton, 1980. Copyright © 1980 by Joan Morrison and Charlotte Fox Zabusky. All rights reserved. Reproduced by permission of the editors.

size, a lawyer with an excellent reputation was a prime target, and particularly with competition among lawyers as there was. So it was one way to eliminate competition very readily, and when a guy doesn't join the Fascist party, he becomes a prime target. Most of the lawyers on Saturdays would go out on the march with the Black Shirts, and my father wouldn't. That was enough to put him in the limelight. He was walking home and they called, "*Avvocato Massoni.*" That means Lawyer Massoni. And he turned around, and as he turned around, they had long sticks just like our policemen carry, and they kept on banging him on the head, and he just put his head down trying to save his face. And he was beaten very badly. Another time they made him drink castor oil in the town square. That was their way of torturing and humiliating people.

You had to be very much afraid at that time. Say, if you were on a train and somebody started making sly remarks about the way the trains are running under fascism or the way the people are starving, you minded your *p*'s and *q*'s, because you knew that that person could very well be an *agent provocateur.* You had to be afraid of your neighbors, you had to be afraid of your maids; you never talked in front of anyone. And every time there was an attempt, for instance, on the life of [Italy's Fascist dictator Benito] Mussolini, the Black Shirts would roam Leghorn and search for the dissidents. And they would just beat them to a pulp. It was not a very pleasant way to live, but in retrospect now, I think it had its fascination. Those were glorious days because there was a true struggle of ideals, you know? . . .

Fleeing Italy

When he knew the war was going to break out, my father took the whole family to Paris. I was walking on the Champs Elysées the day war was declared. That's when the idea crystallized in my father: that the two young male members of our family—I was nineteen and my cousin was seventeen—would come to the United States. We were both medical students, and we would continue medical school. We were of age to serve in the army and we would have been put in the Italian army. And dad said, "No, if you have to fight, you might as well fight where you believe in and go on the winning side and fight for the side that you want to fight for. And if you can continue your studies, fine. And if you can't, then you can serve wherever you are expected to." So we came.

You know, those were tragic times. It was very difficult to get passage. Poland had already been taken, and the Germans were pretty close to Holland. They were expected momentarily to move into Holland. There were an awful lot of Germans in Rotterdam, where we went to get the boat. German Jews particularly. Passages on the boat were

Some Italians fled their native land to escape the rule of dictator Benito Mussolini, seen here with Adolf Hitler.

very difficult to obtain. We had two tickets, and we were with two other young men who also had tickets, and at the last minute, as we were ready to board, there was a family who really—if they had been caught by the Germans, they would have been exterminated. They were German Jews. So we gave them our tickets because we were young men. We felt, "Well, we can always make a go of it." But here was a father, a mother, a daughter, another kid. We gave them our tickets. The boat pulled out and hit a mine in the harbor and sank while we were watching. We could see it. You never know how things will come out. They had thanked us and we had felt generous. . . .

Arrival in America

We took the next boat and it turned out to be the last boat to leave Rotterdam. That boat was like a Grand Hotel. There were refugees from all over Europe: American citizens getting home, Cubans going back to Cuba, Jewish refugees from Germany, and political refugees, young and old, all mixed together. There was the Russian Ballet of Monte Carlo who performed at the Met many times and a band from Cuba that was leaving Europe. Everybody else was older, so they sort of adopted us, and we used to eat with the Cuban band and had it nice. We had good times on that boat. And when we got into New York City everyone was going. Everyone had a place to go. Everybody knew where to go except us. The Cuban boys were getting their instruments, and the Russian Ballet was getting ready to perform at the Metropolitan, and all of a sudden I realized that that was *it*. My last contact with Europe was over. I felt afraid.

We had a little cash and some things we planned to sell—gold cigarette lighters, a fine leather briefcase, that sort of thing. I remember going into a telephone booth and trying to figure out how to dial a hotel and find out if they had a vacancy, in broken English. I said to myself, "This is really going to be rough." We took a cab, and immediately you change your way of thinking. What in Paris cost a few francs, here it looked very little, but then you translate it into francs and Italian lire and you say, "You mean to tell me I've already spent this much just to take a cab? I'm not going to last a week.". . .

We had to get used to eating very little. The food was so different and, of course, we didn't have much money. You'd go into a cafeteria for instance and you'd ask for a sandwich and they'd say, "Rye or white?" and you don't know what they're talking about. What is that? A sandwich is a sandwich. There is no such thing in Italy as rye bread or white bread or whole-wheat bread; it's bread. Bread is bread. Now what is he asking me about the bread? And they say it so fast. I couldn't understand a word. I would just mumble anything. Imitate the first word that he said and if he didn't come back at me with another thing, otherwise I would say anything, you know? Because I just didn't know. And, of course, things that I knew, like spaghetti or macaroni, they were so terrible. But then little by little I learned.

We moved out to Brooklyn, and I remember the delight I used to have in going to delicatessens somewhere there and really loving those hot pastrami sandwiches as if there was no tomorrow. In those days that particular part of Brooklyn was nice. It was cheaper and we liked it. I remember there were small little homes, one after another, and clean streets. Very orderly. The people that rented us a room in their house, they were nice people of Russian origin. Very cordial, really nice. It was like a little bit of the country. And then little by little we began to realize that all the world is alike, you know. We saw some nice people, we saw people that we didn't like as much, but by and large they were friendly. . . .

Learning English

My cousin and I decided to start seriously approaching our problems. First the language. We used to go to Forty-second Street movies for a quarter. We'd watch the same movie three, four, or five times. It was the only way. We would grasp first the ideas of the movie and then concentrate on certain parts to learn the words and meaning. Not with a dictionary, just to get the ear accustomed and then look at it again, and then it would come back a little bit more. By the third or fourth time we would grasp certain expressions. At first it was just a jumble—"Brrrrrr," it sounded like this. Then a little more. We could distinguish a few words here and there, and then little by little from a common sound we could distinguish a few words until they made sense. I had had a couple of years in school of English, but everything was different. It was hard for me to understand the spoken word, and when you don't understand it feels like a jumble. So that was difficult. . . .

But little by little I learned this: First of all I had to take an exam for foreigners in the English language; second, it wasn't automatic to get in a medical school; third, I needed a lot more science courses than I had; and fourth, it would take a lot of money. But my father always said, "To every problem there is a solution." So I worked on the language and I kept applying to medical schools. I applied to seventy-five medical schools. I even applied to the University of Hawaii. And they all turned me down. But I said, "I'm going to be a doctor. I don't care how hard it is or where, but I'm going to be." I was confident that this would take place and I think this confidence was not entirely justified. I found out later, because I know that there are people that are very bright and they belong in medical school and they never made it. So maybe it's good I had this confidence—that this confidence was exaggerated—because then I didn't know any better. I just didn't know any better. Dad had said, "To every problem there's a solution," so it's got to be so because my father couldn't be wrong.

I kept applying and I was fortunate. Harvard accepted me into the Graduate School of Arts and Sciences. They gave me an oral interview and I could hardly speak English. All we talked about was fascism, and I tried to straighten them out, really. They were very attentive. Every time I couldn't find a word during that oral exam, I would say it in English, in Latin, or in Greek—anything, if I could express myself. I thought it would be a handicap, and instead it turned out to be an asset, because they admitted me right there on the spot.

Now I began studying with a dictionary and taking science courses. I took histology, neuropathology, chemistry. I did well in those because language wasn't a factor there. I got an honor grade in neuropathology; so I said, "Well, now it's time." And I went to see my professor. He had an office in the Massachusetts General Hospital. He said, "Well, what can I do for you?"

"I want to go to medical school, because that's what I really want to do."

He said, "Well, I'll be glad to give you a letter of recommendation."

"No, that's not going to help me. There are an awful lot of people with very, very high marks who don't bring credentials from Italy, from a *gymnasium* [preuniversity classical school]—with Greek and Latin and history of art and philosophy, but little in the way of science. I won't stand a chance. There's only one way. It's for you to pick up the phone and say, 'Hey, Joe, I got somebody. You want to take a chance? He doesn't know the language, but he did well in my course and I think he'll work hard. Will you take him?'"

So my professor said, "Okay. Wait outside." I was praying hard and fast. It was a beautiful crisp morning in Boston.

Really beautiful. I remember it as if it was now. Finally he called me in and he said, "Do you have fifty dollars?"

"Sure, I got fifty dollars," which I didn't have.

He said, "Do you know Tufts Medical School? It will take you starting July 1."

So I rushed home, sold the last of my things from Italy for that fifty dollars, and I went in to see the dean of Tufts Medical School. He said, "Do you have the means to support yourself?"

"Oh, money is no object," I said—because I didn't have any, so it couldn't be any object, you know. Once I got that acceptance, that's all I needed, I thought. The rest will come.

Work and School

All the time I was in medical school I worked. I had dozens of jobs. I had three and four jobs at a time. I was a busboy and dog walker. I broadcasted a couple of hours a week for the Office of War Information. I made beds in the university dorm and I washed dishes. Any kind of job, it didn't make any difference to me. It was a step forward and I did it and I never felt degraded by any kind of work.

I was lonely, but I didn't have time to feel lonely because I was so busy working. Everybody would go home for holidays and I would still be there. I had a hot dog at the Wursthaus on Thanksgiving Day because I couldn't afford turkey. I used to feel depressed, but then I used to say, "Don't feel so sorry for yourself. Remember maybe this is your chance. They're going to play and instead you're going to work, and by the time they come back, you'll be that far ahead. And you're handicapped by the language, so you have to make it up by working extra."

Saturday night everybody would go out on a date, and that was the night for me in which I could really study, because I could study all night long, and at five in the morning I would get up and make my rounds with the *New York Times*. I delivered it every Sunday morning. I remember that winter. Boston is cold. The snow would be high. I wasn't used to it either. Remember, I was coming from Italy. I used to say to myself, "Oh, if only the *Times* wasn't so heavy on Sunday."

My daughter's at Radcliffe now. Before she went, she said, "I'm going to miss the *New York Times*." So I got on the phone and ordered it, and it's thrown on her doorstep. I called up and I said, "I want my daughter to get the paper. I want you to deliver it to my daughter, room such-and-such, the *New York Times*, including Sunday. How much should I make the check for?"

My daughter doesn't realize how much it means to me to be able to do that for her. Or when she tells me, "Dad, my tuition is due," to be able to say, "Okay. I've deposited it in your account. Just go to your bank and transfer it." She complains I talk too much about money. She doesn't know what it means to me. When I had to do it, I had to go and give blood transfusions and sell my suitcase and sweaters and shirts and ties in order to pay the tuition. She doesn't realize the pleasure that I have. She gets mad now because I'm talking money to her.

Restrictions on Italian Americans' Civil Liberties During World War II

Vitina Spadaro

The United States entered into World War II in 1941 against the Axis powers of Germany, Japan, and Italy. Concerned about domestic security, American authorities restricted the civil rights of Americans identified as ethnic German, Japanese, or Italian. In 2000 the U.S. Congress passed the Wartime Violation of Italian American Civil Liberties Act to acknowledge that the civil rights of Italian Americans were violated during World War II and to find ways to better protect citizens' civil liberties during times of national emergency. In the following selection excerpted from congressional testimony given in support of the wartime violation act, Vitina Spadaro recounts her childhood memories of the way her Italian American family's life was disrupted by the restrictive acts of the U.S. government. Spadaro and her father were both naturalized American citizens. Despite this fact and their demonstrated loyalty to America, the family was forced to move from their coastal California home to the inland town of Salinas. They gave up the family fishing boat, the source of the family's livelihood, to American government authorities. The boat was later returned in a severely damaged condition. The family lived under a curfew for the duration of the war. Spadaro describes her childhood fear of speaking Italian with her mother in public and her great-

Vitina Spadaro, testimony before the U.S. House Constitution Subcommittee, House Judiciary Committee, October 26, 1999.

est fear of all, being interned in a camp just as Japanese American families had been interned.

This is a story that must be told. It begins when I was a little girl in Italy, listening to grownups about all the wonderful things America stands for: freedom, the opportunity to work. I came here at age seven, and my father said since he was a citizen, I was automatically one too. I was very proud. He said to me, "Here is where we will make our home. We will always obey the laws of this country." Fishing was my father's livelihood. He had his own boat, the *Marettimo*. I always went to school. We had our house on 291 Larkin Street [in Monterey, California].

Betrayal of Italian Americans

All was fine until the war came. I felt betrayed by this country. All I learned in school and believed in was different than what was taking place. Everything changed. We were Italians, and we were looked at as enemies. My mother had to register because she was an alien. She had been going to school in Monterey to get her citizenship, but with the war she had to stop. When orders came for my mother to leave Monterey, I went with my parents to look for a house in Salinas. When we would ask for a place to live, they would ask why we had to move. We told them, and they said, "Are you those Italians from Monterey? You're aliens. We're not renting to you." I felt devastated.

I would say to them, "I'm an American citizen, my father is an American citizen." My father would say, "Keep quiet." But how could they hurt my mother like this? She was crying all the time. When we were getting ready to move to Salinas, there were moving vans all over the neighborhood, and all the women were crying. After we found a place, my father would go back and forth to Monterey, to check the house there, and fish. I was only thirteen and had to move with my mother. I went to Salinas' Washington Junior High.

Then the 8:00 P.M. curfew came. I was always scared when I went shopping with my mother. There was fear because someone could hear me speak Italian with her. There were signs saying not to. We heard on the radio about how they were going to move the Italians. From news at school and from other friends in the same predicament there was fear of the concentration camp. I knew I would have to be locked up if my mother was. When I would come home from school, there was a terrible fear that they had taken my mother, and maybe me too, that they'd be waiting for me.

I remember asking my father, "Why, why, when we didn't break the law, are they doing this to us?" He would say, "There's a war going on. People in command don't know what they're doing."

The Family Fishing Boat

His boat, the *Marettimo*, was a purse seiner. There was a fishing fleet in Monterey, all owned by Italians, all citizens. Then I remember my father saying there was someone from the government who wanted our fishing boats. "What can we do, the government needs our boats," my father said. So he had to deliver his boat to San Francisco, to the Navy. Seventy boats from Monterey were taken; it was a deal agreed to by the boat-owner's association. Being good Italians, they wanted to help the government so they were willing to let the boats go. But up north they had a fishing fleet, mostly Slavonians, and down south, they also had a fishing fleet. I feel the reason they wanted the Monterey boats was because they were Italians. They had to charter boats from up north and bring them down here to fish, to support their families. Why not take the boats up north?

Anyway, after several months, my father was notified

that he could get his boat. He found the boat in bad shape. They had put cannons and guns on it. He was very upset. He asked about the skiff, which was missing. All fishing boats had to have skiffs—they were big enough for a 12-man crew. They told him all the skiffs were destroyed because the Navy had no use for them. My father said, "I need money to get my boat back into condition." They said they'd give him $3,000. He didn't like it, said he'd think it over, because he knew it would take $3,000 to replace the skiff alone. He checked and found he would need much more, maybe $15,000, which he told them. They said, "Either you accept what we give you, or we keep your boat." They forgot boat owners were citizens. My father called home, told my mother about it. She said, "Bring the boat back. We'll do what we can to continue."

So here he was with a boat in poor condition, no skiff, and he had already chartered a boat for the season. He had to tie the *Marettimo* at anchor. A terrific storm came in December. The Coast Guard called to say the boat was in danger. My father was anchored out in a cove, unable to come in. My mother asked me to talk to the Coast Guard, and I said, "Please, see what you can do to save the boat." They refused. The boat was wrecked. The insurance covered very little; most went to try to salvage the boat. Eventually, my father sold the *Marettimo* to a boat builder for next to nothing. Then he had to get a loan, from the Bank of America, to get a new boat. It cost $45,000. Many other fishermen in Monterey had to do the same thing to repair their boats. The Navy fixed up the first three boats they returned, in better shape than before. But the rest, they just had to take it or leave it.

"A Good American Citizen"

My mother and I came home to Monterey in September 1942. But no one complained. Even when the orders came to move out, and no one said we'll help you, it was difficult, but these good Italians just went ahead and obeyed the law. My father, even when he lost his boat, kept on being a good American citizen. This was our country.

I had a lot of anger, though, especially against General [John] DeWitt [responsible for forcing Japanese Americans into internment camps]. I told my teacher, and she encouraged me to write a letter to him. I remember saying I wanted to go back to my home in Monterey. I actually got a response, saying for me to be patient, we'd get home in due time. Which we did. So it was a very difficult time for us. My father lost his life savings to get the new boat. I felt betrayed of everything I believed in. This was an injustice to the Italian people. They came for a better life. They came to work hard, and they had a lot of pride. They didn't expect to take away from the country but to contribute, and they have and still are. But during the war everyone lived in fear. We heard what they were doing to the Japanese. We were always afraid we were going to be next.

CHAPTER 3

From Immigration to Assimilation

COMING TO AMERICA

The Third Generation's Passage into the Middle Class

Humbert S. Nelli

World War II brought many changes to the lives of Italian Americans. At the end of the war returning soldiers found that Congress had passed a law, commonly referred to as the GI Bill of Rights, that provided veterans the resources to get a college education or to acquire a low-interest loan to buy a home. Thousands of Italian Americans took advantage of the opportunities provided by the GI Bill. Earning a degree made it possible for many Italian Americans to move into the professions and to greatly increase their earning power. Families moved from the old ethnic enclaves of the inner cities to the suburbs and began to assimilate into American society. Old community institutions began to decline, and Italian Americans became Italian only on festival days when they returned to the old neighborhoods to celebrate their heritage. In the next selection Humbert S. Nelli surveys the changes in Italian American families following World War II. Nelli is a professor of history at the University of Kentucky at Lexington and is the author of several history books, including *The Business of Crime: Italians and Syndicate Crime in the United States* and *Italians in Chicago, 1880–1930: A Study in Ethnic Mobility.*

Following the end of World War II soldiers, sailors, and other servicemen returned to civilian life and a grateful and

Humbert S. Nelli, *Immigrants to Ethnics: The Italian Americans.* New York: Oxford University Press, 1983. Copyright © 1983 by Humbert S. Nelli. Reproduced by permission of the publisher.

appreciative society. There was strong bipartisan support for Congressional passage, in June 1944, of the Servicemen's Readjustment Act, the so-called G.I. Bill of Rights. "A grateful nation," [historian] Arthur Link has observed, "poured out its resources to help its former servicemen."

The G.I. Bill was the vital element that made it possible for many Italian Americans and also members of other ethnic groups to enter the middle class. Thousands of Italian Americans made use of the G.I. Bill to attend college, most to become the first in their family to receive a degree. The degrees made it possible to qualify for careers in law, medicine, or large business corporations. Ex-servicemen also made use of low-interest loans from the Veterans' Administration (the VA) or from the Federal Housing Administration (the FHA) to leave core-area Little Italys and join other Americans of their generation in the suburbs. One Italian American recalled: "The G.I. Bill gave many of our men the economic ladder to go up and the FHA gave them the money to get out." FHA or VA financing "made it possible to live in a house that had three cubic inches of grass and assured status. If you moved to suburbia, you would finally find the recognition and acceptance from the larger America that the people in the old neighborhood had always wanted." Those who wanted to remain "in the old neighborhood," on the other hand, found that the only source of loan money was "through the building and loans that the ethnics themselves created and that necessitated a one third down payment." This was because, at least until the mid-1960s, both the FHA and VA preferred to loan money for the construction of new housing in suburban areas, not for the purchase of existing structures in the urban core. The latter were considered to be bad risks, in large part because of the presence of what the FHA Operation Manual termed "inharmonious racial or national groups." In other words, increasing numbers of blacks from the rural American South and Spanish-speaking newcomers from Mexico and Puerto Rico during and after World War II flocked into inner-city neighborhoods which, in the view of financial institutions and federal bueaucrats, made the entire core a bad risk for everything except public housing.

Emerging Ethnic Awareness

This fact is ironic because the ethnic consciousness that formed in the black ghettos of American cities during the 1950s and 1960s played a central role in the development of the ethnic awareness that emerged among Italians, Poles, and other white groups in the late sixties and seventies. As one group leader complained in the press [*Fra Noi*] in November 1971: "The revolution of the '60s has seen the blacks achieve some measure of acceptance in their struggle for equal treatment. . . . Is it too much for Italo-Americans to ask for their fair share of human dignity from that same community?" This demand grew out of the conviction that group pride and the application of group pressure enabled blacks to gain benefits that other groups ought to share. Thus journalist Ken Auletta who was a New York City politician in the 1960s and 1970s recalls that "black power demands were followed by community and then ethnic group demands from poor Hispanics, Jews, and Italo Americans."

This is not, of course, what earlier generations of Italian Americans believed was the most effective way to gain acceptance. Previously, many would have fully agreed with observations novelist John Fante made about his immigrant-generation father in a magazine article printed in the late 1930s:

> I look up at him in amazement. Is this man my father? Why, look at him! Listen to him! He reads with an Italian inflection! He's wearing an Italian mustache. I have never

realized it until this moment, but he looks exactly like a Wop. His suit hangs carelessly in wrinkles upon him. Why the deuce doesn't he buy a new one? And look at his tie! It's crooked. And his shoes; they need a shine. And for the Lord's sake, will you look at his pants! They're not even buttoned in front. And, oh damn, damn, damn, you can see those dirty old suspenders that he won't throw away. Say, mister, are you really my father? You there, why you're such a little guy, such a runt, such an old looking fellow! You look exactly like one of those immigrants carrying a blanket? You can't be *my* father.

While the youngsters of Fante's generation typically were ashamed of their stranger-looking parents and tried to hide their Italian origins, *their* children are different. In the homogenized environment of suburbia, Italian Americans of the third generation in search of their self-identity have re-examined the experiences of the immigrant generation and take pride in what their parents abhored: the peasant origins of their grandparents and the miserable living and working conditions they encountered and endured in core-area tenement neighborhoods.

The Move to the Suburbs

Italian Americans have shared fully in the general prosperity the nation has enjoyed since World War II. Movement out of the ethnic districts slowed during the 1930s because of the Depression and during the 1940s because of wartime housing shortages, but by the 1950s the process had accelerated, and the formerly heavy concentrations of Italians in immigrant neighborhoods has thinned out. Thus although Chicago's Near West Side community continues in existence, its population is greatly reduced. The district held an Italian immigrant population of 12,995 in 1920; the same area contained a *combined* total of first- and second-generation Italians of 5,140 in 1960 and only 1,806 ten years later. In Boston's Italian district, the North

End, the population decreased by 45.8 percent between 1950 and 1960, and by 40 percent in the next ten years. The decline, according to [scholar] Spencer Di Scala, is attributable "to younger people and couples moving out of the area." The general tendency has been "for more established persons to move out and for newer arrivals from Italy to take their place.". . .

In [the late 1970s] a new trend has emerged in such communities as Boston's North End and Chicago's Near West Side. While upwardly mobile Italian Americans continue to move out of the colony in search of a better life, non-Italian young upper-middle-class suburbanites are moving in. They are flocking "into the North End (and the surrounding waterfront) because it has become very fashionable to live there. . . . Many of the old buildings are being purchased and renovated by developers." Di Scala finds this process "disturbing" because after the rehabilitation has been completed long-established Italian residents "can no longer afford to pay the high rents" and are forced to move out. . . .

Decline of Community Institutions

Among Italian Americans in the postwar decades traditional immigrant community institutions had, with the exception of the Catholic Church, fallen into disuse. Mutual-benefit societies and the Italian-language press, vibrant and influential institutions during the immigrant era, had by the 1960s come on hard times. A survey of more than three hundred Italian residents of Chicago's Near West Side found that none of the people interviewed belonged to an Italian fraternal organization and none read a foreign-language newspaper, nor did anyone else in their families. Many were not even aware of the existence of the two largest Italian fraternal groups: the Sons of Italy and the Italo-American National Union. A sizable minority claimed to own life-insurance policies, but with American companies. Only the Catholic Church continued to attract support: almost without exception residents claimed membership in one of the three Catholic churches in the area, although religious observance appeared to be more common among the older generation than among their children.

The elderly still obtained news of events in Italy from Italian-language radio broadcasts and from a monthly paper, *Fra Noi*, which regularly printed a summary page in Italian. *Fra Noi* is put out by a Catholic religious order, and during the mid-sixties was the only city publication written about and for Italian Americans. Later, the weekly *L'Italia* was started; by 1979 its circulation had reached 6000. The Italian-language press has been somewhat stronger in the East, where Italian immigrants continue to arrive and congregate. Yet only New York's *Il Progresso Italo-Americano*, which has a national as well as a local edition, publishes daily. *Il Progresso*'s circulation in 1979 was 58,251; the next largest Italian-language paper, the *Italian Echo* of Providence, Rhode Island, a weekly, had a circulation of only 23,000. . . .

The New Family

Third-generation Italian Americans are not only more likely than members of earlier generations to marry outside the ethnic group, they also are more readily disposed to dissolve unsuccessful marriages. Divorce is no longer an unthinkable and unacceptable option.

The contemporary Italian-American family tends to resemble the smaller, more egalitarian, child-centered units typical of the American middle class. Even among the working class the third generation is only "slightly more patriarchal than other lower class families but still strives toward the 'democratic family' ideal." In keeping with the native-American norm, the third-generation Italian-American husband "is likely to have a spouse who bears no resemblance to the old immigrant woman who considered herself entirely dedicated to her husband's wishes and caprices, and he accepts this behavior as proper." Marital roles generally "are divided along sex lines, but there are many areas—including child-rearing and discipline, cooking, cleaning—in which at times the two spouses exchange or complement roles." The family is "decidedly child-centered. The children are deliberately instructed in the ways of the American middle-class." Thus education is highly valued. "Indeed, in reaction to the lack of education in the family background, the parents are often obsessively concerned with the success of the children in school." If they do not already live in the suburbs one of the family's goals is to move, generally to an industrial suburb located adjacent to the city. Nevertheless, contact still is maintained with parents, grandparents, and friends still living in the old neighborhood.

Italian Food and Festivals

Suburbanite Italian Americans also still drive to core-area neighborhood stores on shopping expeditions for olive oil, salami, cheese, artichokes, pepperoni, and other "authentic" food unavailable in the shopping-center supermarket. They also return to "the old neighborhood" to participate in religious festivals and celebrations. In New York City the main social event of the year for the various Italian colonies is the six-day Festival of San Gennaro, celebrated each September along Mulberry Street, on Manhattan's Lower East Side. Each day and night the narrow, booth-lined street is choked with milling crowds of people. The principal pastime is the patronage of canopied booths bulging with pizza, sausage-and-eggplant sandwiches, zeppolo, lemon ices, tortoni, torrone, balloons, parasols, dolls, hats, chances on stuffed animals, chances on automobiles. Neighborhood vegetable stores, cheese shops, restaurants, and bars also enjoy a thriving business as do Ferris wheels temporarily erected on parking lots. While San Gennaro is a Neapolitan *festa* [festival] the descendants of Italians from other provinces and non-Italians are all welcome to participate in the festivities, to watch the fireworks displays, and to observe the procession and high mass on the sixth day which mark the culmination of the celebration.

Italians and others alike flock to the San Gennaro, San Rocco, Santa Rossilia, and other feast days from remote parts of New York City and its suburbs and even from neighboring states. Many are attracted by the wide variety and high quality of the food in stalls and local restaurants, little realizing or even caring that what they consume is not typical peasant fare. Food is also the main attraction at ethnic festivals held annually, if not more frequently, in various Eastern and Middle-Western cities. One such celebration, a "Festa Italiana," was held on Navy Pier in Chicago from August 21 to 23, 1981. A crowd estimated at 100,000 "came from all Chicago neighborhoods, from the suburbs, and beyond" to observe an idealized vision of life "in the old days" in core-area Italian neighborhoods. "The entire south end of Navy Pier was transformed into one gigantic Italian neighborhood of another era. . . . The food stands emitting aromas of Italian cooking assailed you at every step." The crowd had a choice of home-made pasta, baked clams, stuffed aritchokes, fried zucchini, fried calamari, and "Italian sausage with peppers, Italian ices, cannoli, cookies and other delicacies." The festival, according to the chairman of the sponsoring organization, celebrated "Italian-American life and provided a glimpse of our culture."

The Godfather Reflects Changes in Italian American Culture After World War II

Marianna De Marco Torgovnick

Mario Puzo's novel *The Godfather* is about an American Mafia family led by an Italian immigrant, Vito Corleone. The novel, first published in 1969, spent many weeks on the *New York Times* best-seller list. Two years later, a trilogy of films, also entitled *The Godfather* (*I, II, and III*) based on Puzo's novel and directed by Francis Ford Coppola, began appearing in movie theaters. The *Godfather* films have been called the greatest gangster films ever made. Puzo's novels and Coppola's films permanently linked Italian Americans to organized crime in the minds of many Americans. In the following excerpt, Marianna De Marco Torgovnick points out that one of the central issues in Puzo's novel concerns the changes in the Italian American family after World War II. Immigrants such as the Corleone family in the novel sought higher education for their children. However, this education led the new generation of Italian Americans to abandon much of their traditional culture as they assimilated into American life. Torgovnick also argues that the novel's portrayal of men as strong and women as inferior reflects an aspect of Italian American culture that resisted change. *The Godfather* emphasizes the idea of male power and rejects the idea of college and careers for women. Torgovnick, a professor of English at Duke Uni-

Marianna De Marco Torgovnick, *Crossing Ocean Parkway: Readings by an Italian American Daughter*. Chicago: The University of Chicago Press, 1994. Copyright © 1994 by Marianna De Marco Torgovnick. All rights reserved. Reproduced by permission of the publisher and the author.

versity, is the author of several books, including *Gone Primitive: Savage Intellects, Modern Lives.*

The Godfather gives us the hum and buzz of Italian American culture, quite apart from its portrayal of the distinct and much smaller subculture of the Mafia. Specifically, it portrays Italian American culture in the decade from 1945 to 1955. This decade initiated massive changes in Italian American life, among them the increased presence of Italian Americans in writing, publishing, and universities. Like historical novels, *The Godfather* shows how "the past is the concrete precondition of the present" [according to Georg Lukác]. It shows how Italian Americans got from their relative cultural isolation in 1945 into the mainstream.

In 1945, as the novel opens, Michael Corleone is a returned war veteran, attending Dartmouth College, then as now a bastion of WASP culture. Attendance at college presumes his separation from the family business—even if that business were to be the production of olive oil rather than crime. It has further encouraged a love affair with a Protestant daughter of New England, since college-educated Italian American girls, like the novel's Lucy Mancini, are rare. The Italian American community is aware of these changes: Michael's entrance to Dartmouth (as opposed to the more expected, because local, City University, New York University, or Columbia) translates, in the community's terms, into having "left his father's house." [Character] Kay Adams appears to the group a "washed-out rag of an American girl," her manner "too free for a maiden" Lucy's morals are suspect as "thoroughly Americanized." In Bakhtinian [Russian critic Mikhail Bakhtin] terms, the values and the language of the traditional Italian American infiltrate the novel. To people outside the Italian American community, the distinction between Italian and American would seem spurious, especially since Lucy is, like most younger guests at the wedding, American-born. To outsiders, attending college would seem natural, even desirable, with a college education implying nothing about a young woman's "reputation."

Education and Americanization

The boom in higher education in the decade following Sputnik[1] would open the world of scholarships and degrees to Italian American children. I was part of that generation; Lucy Mancini and Michael Corleone represent the wave of the future. In the novel, the brave new world of education is welcomed, even courted. Michael Corleone, like his father Vito, desires the Americanization of his children because it will dictate their exit from the subculture of the Mafia. As the first Godfather tells his cohorts, "Some of you have sons who are professors, scientists, musicians, and you are fortunate." What the novel does not say, but what lurks within its pages, is that the process of Americanization, carried to its logical conclusion, would represent the end of Italian American culture as it had existed in the prewar decades. It would mean intermarriages like Michael's with Kay, or, even more typically, like Lucy's with Jules Segal. It would mean moving away from the old neighborhoods, establishing cross-country networks of family that minimize closeness and reduce the frequency of family gatherings for dinner that is a hallmark of Italian American culture. *The Godfather* chronicles a moment when Italian Americans—as something quite separate, I must stress, from the Mafia—were assimilating with the majority culture.

The Chinese have a curse that runs something like "May you get what you wish." For Vito Corleone, the curse

---

1. Sputnik was the world's first artificial satellite, launched by the Soviet Union in 1957.

if fulfilled would have meant the passing of his empire from the family as his sons entered the mainstream of American life, becoming part of the world the novel calls the "pezzonovanti," and the sixties called "the military-industrial complex." The dialect and customs of the Sicilians would be displaced by the Florentine Italian taught in universities and by the homogenizing forces of American suburbia, so similar whether in New York, California, Illinois, or North Carolina. Less progressive than Vito Corleone, [Mario] Puzo's mother was baffled by her son's literary ambitions, and she urged him to work instead for the railroads in Hell's Kitchen, an immigrant neighborhood. My own mother could not understand my desire to go to college, thinking that I should instead become a secretary. She trusted that job's financial security and tendency to be relinquished upon motherhood. She rightly sensed (I see now in retrospect) that college would remove me from her world. *The Godfather* thus captures a key point of transition for Italian Americans and the ambivalence often surrounding the idea of college until well into the 1960s.

Traditional Gender Roles

Vito Corleone speaks of sons who are musicians, scientists, professors—not of daughters. In the same way, as late as 1993, [writer] Gay Talese discussed the situation of Italian American writers without mentioning a female other than Camille Paglia [scholar]—and even her very briefly. Like Talese's article, Vito Corleone's speech reflects a significant part of Italian American culture—its emphasis on males and denigration of females. The novel's opening masterfully and subtly establishes the relative spheres of men and women.

The Godfather begins not with the direct presentation of the title character but with a series of indirect approaches to him. In this it rivals other narrative examples, such as the *Odyssey* and *Madame Bovary*, whose openings also delay the presentation of the main character. The novel begins with three vignettes about Italian American men with problems—the undertaker Amerigo Bonasera, the singer Johnny Fontane, and the baker Nazorine. Although the three come from different social strata, each has a problem with the customs, laws, or bureaucracies of the majority culture, and each reaches an identical conclusion: that the Old World mechanisms of the Godfather can help when the institutions of the New World have failed. This is, indeed, the primary point of the opening vignettes.

But they have another point as well. When one looks to the root of each man's problem, one finds a woman— Bonasera's daughter who has taken up with American boys; Fontane's second wife, an actress, a non-Italian, and a "tramp"; Nazorine's "hot number" of a daughter, who requires prompt marrying to the Italian prisoner of war assigned to her father's shop. Each man's trouble comes from his association with women. The novel continues this pattern, most crucially in Sonny's vulnerability on the night he is killed racing to rescue his sister.

Responding to Fontane, the Godfather expressly makes the point that men ought not to take women too seriously. What is Johnny to do? In his most passionate declaration in the novel, the Godfather tells Johnny that he must "start by acting like a man . . . 'LIKE A MAN!'" He warns Johnny not to "let women dictate your actions . . . [because] they are not competent in this world, though certainly they will be saints in heaven while we men burn in hell." Most of all, he urges Johnny to cultivate the value of male friendships, urging upon him his power to help his boyhood friend, Nino.

The novel reinforces the Don's sense of woman's place in multiple ways. The action proper begins with a wedding, as Connie does what good Italian girls are supposed to do:

marries a fellow Italian (albeit a worthless non-Sicilian), transferring her father's power over her to her husband, a power with which even Don Corleone will not interfere. For that wedding, the Corleone women cook, though their immense wealth might free them from such menial duties. Above all, women are not to know, and not to ask, about "business." That is the key lesson that Kay must learn as a wife. The need for women's ignorance is more pressing in the world of crime than in others, but the Mafia world is a microcosm of Italian American society in this regard. Men and male lines of affiliation count; women play a secondary and supportive role, a role more or less separate from their men's.

In its traditional attitudes towards women, Italian American culture magnified the more general views of postwar American culture. While writing this essay, I chanced to see the old movie *Father of the Bride* and was reminded of how pervasively and consistently the fifties iterated and reiterated lessons about men's and women's proper roles. But the strong patriarchal models embedded in traditional Italian life served more than a representational role in *The Godfather*, which was published in 1969—not in the forties or fifties. Nineteen sixty-nine was a year of bra-burnings and demonstrations, of the movement then called "women's liberation," when one hot issue was whether to use "Ms." or "Miss" and "Mrs." The movement was a frequent topic of conversation, soon to be a common subject on popular television situation comedies like *All in the Family*, *The Mary Tyler Moore Show*, and *Maude*. Nineteen sixty-nine was a year when it was possible to be called, with no irony intended, "A women's lib dame." While it is difficult to say for sure, one suspects that the novel's treatment of women had a special appeal in 1969 for an audience uneasy about women's new assertiveness. By portraying the macho world of the Mafia, the novel served as both fantasy and wish fulfillment, and as a way of coping with changing patterns of gender relationships.

The emphasis on male power so pervasive in *The Godfather* has had distinct and in many ways undesirable consequences for Italian American culture, as well as consequences in my own life that make me especially sensitive to it. When, in 1983, the *New York Times Magazine* featured a cover story on Italian Americans' entry into powerful positions, it was striking to me that most of the portraits were of men. Almost all the Italian American women of achievement were traditional enough to be married and to have taken their husbands' names. But they were not, by and large, married to Italian Americans. As a female born in Brooklyn in 1949, my own attitudes towards being Italian American are considerably more ambivalent than those of males I know. In fact, the first time I used my family name (as middle name) in a published piece was when I originally published this essay; before that, I associated my Italian heritage with hostility to my desire to read, teach, and write. It is difficult to prove, except by anecdotal evidence, how strongly Italian American culture in the period and place covered by Puzo's novel resisted the idea of college and careers for women, even while beginning to entertain those ideas for men. . . .

Other hums and buzzes of Italian American life inform the novel. Sick friends and relatives, especially friends of one's parents, must be visited in the hospital. Frequent phone calls to the family are a requirement, their cessation an insult. Honor, especially male honor as vested in females, has paramount value; "respect" is a primary good, which must be shown in a variety of appropriate ways. The novel shows these aspects of Italian American culture at large as clearly as it reveals, more obviously and sensationally, the hum and buzz of Mafia life: the organization of regimes, the conduct of wars, the rules governing civilians, the meaning of a dead fish sent as a message. The Mafia rules have gotten the most attention from reviewers and the general public, and for good reason. Learning how to survive in an exotic world has been an established lure of the novel from *Robinson Crusoe* through the novels of Louis L'Amour. But one learns, from this novel, much that is as natural as breathing to Italian Americans. Along with Kay Adams, non-Italian readers learn what Italian Americans know by acculturation, such as "how important it was to do such things [as visit the hospital] if you wanted to get along with the old Italians."

From an Italian Village to the American Space Program

Al Santoli

Al Santoli entered the United States as an infant in 1921, sailing by steamship from a tiny village near Naples, Italy, with his mother and brother to meet his father who had immigrated one year earlier. In many ways Santoli's life exemplifies the archetypical Italian immigrant's experience. In this interview with his journalist son, Santoli describes a hardworking but happy childhood. He has good memories of life, even in the depths of the Great Depression when every member of the family had to work hard. Santoli enlisted in the military and served in World War II, and like so many other returning veterans, began a career using skills he had learned while in the military. He married and advanced his career, and as his income increased and children came along, Santoli moved his family to the Cleveland suburbs. In 1963 Santoli had an opportunity to work on the National Aeronautics and Space Administration's (NASA) Apollo program. He shares his thoughts on beginning his life in a small mountain town in Italy and going on to help send Americans to outer space.

When I arrived in this country from Italy in 1921, everybody came by boat. There were no transatlantic commercial airlines. We wouldn't have been able to afford the price of a ticket even if there was. My father came first, in 1920,

Al Santoli, *New Americans: An Oral History: Immigrants and Refugees in the U.S. Today.* New York: Viking Penguin, Inc., 1988. Copyright © 1988 by Al Santoli. Reproduced by permission of Viking Penguin, a division of Penguin Group (USA) Inc. and the author.

to establish himself. He came through Ellis Island in New York Harbor with thousands of other immigrants from all parts of Europe.

The United States was still a very young country, still growing. Big cities like New York, Boston, and Cleveland needed the strong backs and craft skills of immigrants. My mother's father was a co-owner of his own construction business in Cleveland. Dad and all of the men from my hometown who were helping to build the city didn't make much money. But they sent enough back to Italy to support their families.

I was just a baby when my mother packed up all the worldly possessions she could carry to join my father in America. We made the boat journey with many other Old Country relatives who were leaving their farms behind for what they hoped would be a better life. We landed in Boston and took a train for six hundred miles through New York and Pennsylvania to Cleveland. This was my mother's first experience of a big industrial city. My four-year-old brother, Tony, and I were too young to have any real fear or expectations.

Until my father found a house of our own, we stayed in my Uncle Jim DeMateo's home, which was already crowded with his wife and kids, plus a few boarders. Can you imagine a dozen people in a single-family house? We only stayed a short while, until Pa rented a place on 105th Street near Cedar Avenue. In the neighborhood, the only people who spoke English were the black people and some Italian kids who had been living there for a long while. At home we spoke only Italian. But by the time I started kindergarten, I knew English from playing with kids on the street.

Growing Up in Cleveland

In 1927, when I was six, we moved to Angelus Street, on the Southeast Side. It was called the Corlett neighborhood, because the streetcar ran on Corlett Avenue. Very few people had cars. Our milk was delivered by large wagons pulled by horses. Fruit-and-vegetable peddlers and the "paper-rags" man also drove horse wagons. He would ride down the street shouting in a deep voice, "Paay-per rags, Paay-per rags!" He would take old papers, clothes, and scrap materials that people didn't need, then sell them to earn his living.

Cleveland was divided into ethnic areas. But a few neighborhoods, like Corlett, were a mixture of many immigrant nationalities. The block I lived on was mostly Italian. But going east was a mixture of Italians, a lot of Bohemians, some Polish families and Slovenians. Also in the neighborhood were some Americans—English, some Germans, and a few Irish. And a few blocks away was a small black community which had been there before we arrived. The Jewish neighborhood was up toward Union Avenue into the Kinsman area.

Most people in the neighborhood didn't speak English as a first language. On the street, nobody ever felt self-conscious about speaking in their own ethnic tongue. If I was out in public with my mother, I'd talk Italian. On the streetcar, you'd hear all these people—Bohemian, Slovak, or Polish—speaking their own language. The only time people used English was with somebody from a different ethnic group. . . .

Becoming American Citizens

At home, we still spoke only Italian. But we considered ourselves to be Americans, too. The government wasn't rushing immigrants to become citizens. People like my dad did that gradually, as they became more adjusted to American life. He wanted to study, to learn about his new country and be prepared. He went to a night class to study for his citizenship test. He took me with him to translate, then he would study at home. I was thirteen years old when Dad got his citizenship papers in 1933.

My brother Tony and I automatically became citizens when my father was sworn in. My brothers Sam, Ray, and Pat and my sister, Elvira, were born here, so they were Americans from birth. My mother was required to get her own separate citizenship papers, but she never did, because she never learned to read or write in English. It never bothered her. She was just as American as we were.

In Italy, children were encouraged to begin working on the farm as soon as they were strong enough to walk. But my father always wanted us to stay in school. He had some education when he was a kid, so he knew how important it was to learn. I wanted to quit school after ninth grade to help support the family. I had just finished at Nathan Hale Junior High. Some of my friends had already dropped out and were working. I told my father, "Dad, I'm going to paint the house, and then maybe I'll go to work." He kept telling me, "I think you should go back to school. I don't expect you to drop out."

I finished painting the house anyway, but three weeks later I reluctantly started classes at John Adams High, which was right across the street from my home. Today I'm thankful that Dad convinced me to change my mind.

World War II

After graduation, I couldn't afford college. It was 1939, the tail end of the Depression. Work was still hard to come by. I put in applications at stores and factories all over town . . . and I mean *all over*. But I couldn't find work. Finally I was hired by an optical company. I went from the mail room into the shop, where I learned to be an eyeglass-lens cutter and grinder. But Pearl Harbor was bombed, and the United States entered the war. Right away, I volunteered into the service. In my neighborhood, most young men went into the military. I never saw one ethnic family take exception. Everyone wanted to do their part. Regardless if they had to go overseas to fight against their own people.

I found that, once immigrants like my dad took the citizenship oath, they were sincere. When they say, "I pledge allegiance to the United States," they meant that. When the American army invaded Italy, many of our soldiers were Italian Americans. They went right in and did what they had to do. . . .

The army sent me to the Aeronautical Institute in Lincoln, Nebraska, to learn airplane-engine mechanics. After I qualified on B-17, B-24, and B-29 bomber aircraft, I was sent to Guam Island in the Pacific. I was made a crew chief and inspector in the 20th Air Force. Our planes did bombing missions against Japan. In my unit, there were people from all over the United States. I learned a lot about life from my buddies. The whole experience greatly expanded my ideas about what I could do in life.

World War II changed a lot of things for my generation of immigrants. Not the old folks so much, but the young. We came home from the military with much higher confidence and expectations. We all bought cars and branched out away from our ethnic boundaries.

Marriage and a New Job

I was discharged from the service on Christmas Eve, 1945. My steady girl, Fay [Serafina Ambrogio], was waiting for me. We were married three months later, on March 2, 1946. We were twenty-five years old. Like many of my friends and relatives, I broke with the old Italian tradition of living close to my parents and moved to another area of Cleveland, which was closer to where I worked. Convenience was only part of the reason. Most young couples wanted to live in better neighborhoods, where their kids would have a better environment.

I found a job at Cleveland Airport as a mechanic and inspector for the Air Force Reserve Training Command. In the postwar years, the government maintained a pretty good-sized reserve, because nobody knew what would happen in various parts of the world. When the Russians blockaded Berlin, some of my buddies were called back into active duty. The air force had to drop supplies into Berlin to break the siege. And later on, the Korean War broke out.

At the airport, I worked on aircraft and engine maintenance five days a week. I worked overtime whenever I could. My first child . . . was born in June 1949. And in 1950, just before the air base was closed, my second child, Gloria, was born. Because of the kids, my wife and I decided to move to a larger home back in my old neighborhood. When my air-force reserve job was phased out, I was offered a position in the Navy Department's Bureau of Aeronautics.

I was assigned to a massive factory, Thompson Products, which became a branch of TRW in Cleveland. My job was the inspection and quality control of aircraft parts. My supervisors were naval officers, but TRW was making aircraft equipment, like jet engines, for all branches of the military. My responsibility to the government was to assure that all parts manufactured met contract requirements. My ultimate concern was the safety of our boys in the service, who would use these items in their aircraft. Without my division's signature to guarantee quality, nobody at that shop would get paid.

For the next thirty years, I worked as a representative of the Defense Supply Agency in private industry. I attended eighteen different colleges and schools and earned the equivalent of degrees in chemical and mechanical engineering, and in industrial management. In my job, I had to follow the manufacturing process from the acquisition of raw materials to the finished assembly of the product. I had to be able to inspect the entire process.

Move to the Suburbs

Even though I was moving up in education and job responsibility, my wife and I and our three children—Albert, Gloria, and Donna—stayed in the old neighborhood until 1961. By that time, just about everyone I grew up with had moved to the new suburbs that were being built just outside the city. Cleveland's ethnic neighborhoods were breaking up. My family was becoming part of the American melting pot.

My brother Sam and I both married Italian girls. But my brother Tony married a Hungarian, and my brother Ray married a Polish girl from the neighborhood. All of our wives came from first-generation families from the Old Country. Their parents were strictly ethnic.

My sister, Elvira, married a Polish refugee named Stanley. He worked in the steel mills. And my youngest brother, Pat, was the first in our family to earn a college degree. He met his wife, Mary, a red-haired Irish nurse, while he was getting his master's degree at the Chrysler Institute in Michigan.

My dad didn't object to who we married, as long as the couples were happy together. He said, "We all struggle, but the main thing in life is health and happiness." That's how it went. The family is no longer a hundred percent Italian; we're a mixed group. My son, Al, married a Vietnamese. I accept that. As long as they get along, that's fine. . . .

My wife and I have been living in the same house here in South Euclid for twenty-six years now. This suburban area was a forest when I was a kid. When we decided to move from the old neighborhood, it was because the three kids were becoming teen-agers and they were still sleeping in the same room. We needed a bigger house, and the neighborhood was going downhill.

Financially, the move was a leap of faith. I was paid a government salary, which in those days was not more than $12,000. We looked at a number of housing developments that were being built before we decided on South Euclid. When we moved in, the street wasn't even paved. The whole area was covered with mud. Each house on our street was painted white, with six rooms and a basement. But each buyer could choose their own style of roof and interior design. We told the builder, "Make ours look exactly like the model house," with a pink roof. And the contractor did us two favors. First, he lowered the kitchen cupboards, because we are short people. And, to save us some money, he allowed my father and Uncle Angelo to help me put in our own concrete driveway and build my own garage. . . .

NASA's Apollo Program

In 1963, NASA began the Apollo Program to send a spacecraft to the moon. In this new phase of space exploration, I was assigned to the Space Program Division at TRW. NASA reviewed my background and assigned me to be their representative. I started working by myself, but in a short period of time I became the supervisor of a whole division. We were doing research development and production for items and systems to be used in lunar spacecraft in the Apollo Program.

The work was incredibly challenging both in the areas of scientific progress being made and in the speed and demands of our production schedule. My division's responsibility was to make sure that quality wasn't sacrificed. Each and every item that came from our shop had to be at least 99.9 percent reliable. As you know from the recent space-shuttle tragedy,[1] we couldn't afford even the slight-

---

1. The *Challenger* space shuttle exploded in 1986.

est error in any item that went into a spacecraft. . . .

All of us in the program realized that we were on the cutting edge of history. Whenever a spacecraft went up successfully, we were elated. I felt a deep pride that, to this day, I have a difficult time expressing.

As the Apollo Program advanced toward the first-manned flight to the moon, we didn't have time to savor our previous accomplishments. I remember being invited down to Florida to observe one of the space shots. But I was a supervisor of both inspection and quality assurance in my division. The program was charging ahead. So I wasn't allowed to go. Instead, I chose one of my team members to go to Florida in my place.

To prepare for the moon landing, the third item we produced was the exhaust cone that allows a space capsule to land on a planet. The cone, which is around four feet long, is located on the bottom of the space capsule. It contains the rockets necessary for descent onto a planet's surface.

On July 20, 1969, it was an incredible feeling to watch the Apollo 11 space shot on television as our astronaut Neil Armstrong walked on the moon. I thought of the small farm town I came from in the mountains of Italy, where people were lucky to attend elementary school and didn't even have plumbing or running water in their homes.

Dressing to Assimilate and Dressing to Have Fun

Maria Laurino

In this excerpt from *Were You Always Italian?* Maria Laurino explores her mother's anxiety about avoiding the fashions of lower-class Italian Americans. Her mother wanted to dress her daughter in the styles that would help the family assimilate into refined American society. Laurino uses the example of two Italian designers with completely different styles to illustrate the competing ideals of some Italian Americans. On the one hand, northern Italian Giorgio Armani offers the classical, understated style that Maria Laurino's mother sought for her daughter. Contrasting with Armani's elegant look is the colorful Gianni Versace, whose southern Italian designs teeter between the audaciously chic and the boorish *gavone*—or lower class, as Laurino deems the Versace look. Laurino's mother is dismayed to see that her daughter feels comfortable in the flamboyant and sexy Versace designs and wears them as happily as she does Armani's. Laurino, a journalist and essayist based in New York, concludes that the two designers are the yin and yang of Italian American fashion and that she does not want to choose between them.

At the corner of Madison Avenue and Sixty-eighth Street [New York City] stand a pair of buildings that once told the story of contemporary fashion through the vision of two

Maria Laurino, *Were You Always Italian? Ancestors and Other Icons of Italian America*. New York: W.W. Norton & Company, 2000. Copyright © 2000 by Maria Laurino. Reproduced by permission of W.W. Norton & Company, Inc.

Italians, one born in the genteel "civic" north, the other from the rugged "uncivic" south of Italy. In a simpler time perhaps, before the designer Giorgio Armani moved into his colossal flagship store a few blocks away, before Gianni Versace opened his own fashion palace on Fifth Avenue and ultimately became a household name because of his brutal murder, these two competed for customers, staking out like feuding neighbors their starkly different stylistic territory. The pull and tug of these men, archrivals, master weavers of myth, reminds me of my youth and the role that clothes played in our household. Not that we knew anything about haute couture when I was growing up. But we did know something about good taste and bad taste.

Class Division in Fashion

Above the red brick entrance to the old Armani boutique is a large airy window in the shape of an arch; it resembles a church window, simple and Protestant, a fitting image for the northern Italian often thought of as the high priest of Milanese fashion. To wear the name Giorgio Armani is to bear an imprimatur of luxury and distinction. To enter an Armani shop is to step into the land of taste, a subdued world where shades of beige quietly rule, and in their elegance and beauty conquer.

Next door, the charcoal gray Versace boutique is embellished with sixteen faux Corinthian columns, each crowned with a silver cornice. The Versace window display, always a kaleidoscope of colors, one spring season featured mannequins draped in bright orange, accessorized with matching-color patent leather bags and shiny spike-heeled shoes; these were fiery warriors next to Armani's neutral goddesses. Showy gewgaws adorned the clothes inside; Versace's gold Medusa-head emblem fastens belts, buttons sweaters, and clamps purses shut.

Gianni Versace made an extraordinary career for himself by breaking the rules of fashion, openly defying what Roland Barthes called the "taboo of an aesthetic order," tweaking the tasteful upturned nose of Armani clothes. As Barthes explained in his book *The Fashion System*, "the structural definition of bad taste is linked to this variant: vestimentary depreciation most often occurs through a profusion of elements, accessories and jewels." Or as *Vogue* editor in chief Anna Wintour once put it: "Versace was always sort of the 'mistress' to Armani's wife."

Armani was said to have grumbled about the direction of Italian fashion led by Versace, a trend that some of their colleagues playfully labeled "the good taste of bad taste." But it would be impossible to understand the source of the Armani-Versace rivalry without recognizing that the style of both designers was derived in part from the contradictory outlook of a country deeply divided by class.

My guardians of fashion, my mother and my aunt, would never have made a Versace-like mistake. They would not have worn a bright orange dress with matching patent leather sandals or overdecorated sweaters, sure signs of lower-class Italian-American taste. I would become their model, and they would dress me to look delicate, refined, a picture of good taste.

For many years, my mother and my aunt divided up the duty of dressing me. My aunt took the first decade, my mother watched over the next two. My aunt, a widow in her forties, lived alone in a small apartment and spent most of her paycheck from a clerical job at Western Electric on clothes for herself. She also delighted in dressing her brother's child, and my earliest clothes memories are a swirl of pastels: baby pink, blue, and yellow, the colors of my Easter suits, light wools that hung tentatively on my tiny body, as if the sheep were surprised by the tender age of their new home. Dresses, jackets, skirts, and blouses. Soft cottons, cool wools, cuddly bouclés. . . .

The *Gavone* Outfit

I can recall best one outfit of my mother's: a khaki-colored suit worn with either a plain black or white scoop-necked cotton shirt. She believed in buying "one nice thing," a finely made suit that could be used many times, rather than several cheaper items. Minimalism guided her choices because she feared excess, afraid as she was of looking Italian-American, or *gavone* (pronounced "gah-vone"). *Gavone*, which we used as both adjective and noun, was southern Italian dialect derived from the Italian word *cafone*, or ignorant person. The word meant to us—if one can ever interpret precisely the variable nuances of dialect—low-class. (I didn't realize until years later that *cafone* was the label northern Italians used to mock poor southerners.) *Gavone* outfits combined a sexiness and tackiness that left me awestruck in their excessive splendor.

I had an early encounter with this look as a child at a cocktail party my parents gave prior to a church event. One relative entered our house wearing a tight orange cardigan with a plunging V-neck, a gold cross that dangled between her breasts, clinging black pants, and high-heeled sandals. "That's quite a sweater," my mother laughed nervously, and she did seem to like the cardigan despite its audaciousness. I stood close to this relative for most of the evening, impressed by her full figure, admiring the way her body looked, but disturbed that she had worn this outfit to a gathering attended by a priest. She had Gianni Versace in her bones before the designer ever sold his first pair of skintight pants.

Italian-American clothes were colorful and baroque, often worn by women with jet black hair piled high on the head: tops in turquoise, chartreuse, shocking pink, purple, and coral (an especially popular color at weddings) and clashing pants; dresses dripping with brocades; gold shoes. Like any adolescent who follows fashion trends as if they were the Holy Grail, for years I amused myself flipping through magazines trying to determine that fine line between *gavone* and chic. Beautiful models wore raging reds, shocking pinks, and deep purples, yet those same colors could create that over-the-top Italian-American look. How would I know if I was *gavone* or chic?

Today it amuses me when a design that fits my childhood image of Italian-American taste is labeled haute couture. Yet many of the top designers are Italian, some came from the poorest regions of southern Italy, and how else is fashion created but from memory, the palette of colors, textures, and objects appropriated from one's youth? . . .

Dressing to Assimilate

Because clothes played such a large part in my mother's anxieties about becoming an American, I'm sure that her mixed feelings about leaving my early dressing to my aunt were compounded by her own fear of having to shop for me. "Your sister spoiled her. She got used to good things," my mother would say to my father, who knew that there was no acceptable answer.

"And now we have to buy her nice clothes," she'd conclude to the air. My mother understood that the choice of what to wear could allow you to be something you are not, that fabric and style could transcend class labels, providing the essential threads for a Pygmalion tale. My aunt had the perfect arrangement, according to my mother's fantasy of the single woman's life: she spent very little money on housing, living in a small apartment in an urban area of New Jersey; her success was measured by the clothes she wore in the world.

My mother's sensitivity to the transformative power of clothes was part and parcel of her second-generation instinct to assimilate, and like most children of immigrants, she juggled the difficulties of leaving the Old World to adapt to the New. While she loved her parents, they spoke with a heavy accent and looked like Italian immigrants. Her responsibility to act like a dutiful daughter and her desire to adopt the image of an American suburban housewife and mother could be mutually exclusive, and she lacked the confidence—or the ability to create the *bella figura* [beautiful figure—to look good]—needed to pull off the latter. In trying to abandon the stereotype of the Italian—the greaseball, the *gavone*—mixed messages abounded in our household. My mother wanted to maintain traditions, keep the spirit of our humble origins, but at the same time reject a look that we labeled lower-class.

If ancestry could be masked in the weave of a classic style, then her daughter, educated and well dressed, could achieve dreams beyond my mother's reach. But clothes choices need validation, and my mother, isolated and alone in our house, was ill at ease shopping in a department store. "I don't trust my taste," she said, explaining that she envied women who always knew what they wanted. She would dither and nervously wander among the racks, and ultimately feel helpless until she found a saleswoman to affirm the choices in her hand. . . .

Versace's Southern Italian Style

Gianni Versace was the fashion world's great success story. Born the son of a dressmaker from Reggio di Calabria, by the time of his death he had reportedly built an $800 million empire. He was inspired by, and dressed, many muses, including a vampy Madonna, a curvaceous Elizabeth Hurley, and a royally sensual Princess Di. Versace left southern Italy by the age of twenty to design costumes for the theater, and early on in his career he pronounced his clear differences with the reigning king of Italian fashion, Giorgio Armani.

I looked up what the *New York Times* fashion pages had said about both men over the years: "The Armani style is classic and subdued, as opposed to Versace's more flamboyant, obviously sexy look.". . . .

While the blue-eyed Giorgio Armani, born in Piacenza, an hour away from Milan, grew up surrounded by upper-class Italian style, the nearest capitals for the young Versace would have been Naples, hundreds of miles north, and Palermo, farther south, both considered by northerners to be embarrassments of corruption and decay, and, until designers like Gianni Versace and Dolce & Gabbana came on the scene, the last places to look for inspiration to dress the elegant fashion consumer.

Versace was surrounded by the tastes of southern Italy. It is the taste of poor and working-class people; it is Barthes's "profusion of elements," the composition of bad taste. Bright Mediterranean colors, the earthy sensuality of peasants, the excessive pageantry of the religious south, and a baroque style that rejected simplicity as a metaphor for the Teutonic, northern way of life were images a young Versace would have internalized. . . .

The *gavone* Italian-American look had to have originated in the tastes of southern Italy, carried from one generation to the next. As Gianni Versace rose to the highest echelons of the fashion world, he blotted out his rustic past but achieved success by using attributes of peasant style in his designs. . . .

Fashion writers often described Versace as subversive, yet to me his styles always felt familiar, vaguely comforting, coming from roots that I know. If fashion has historically been a way to enhance and solidify social status—at least, that's what we hoped for in our household—Versace changed the game: he internalized the taste of the poor, drawing on the influences of southern Italy to create a multimillion-dollar empire. Perhaps that's the subversion, the fact that he had turned haute couture on its head with designs that might be called *basse* [low fashion] couture. . . .

The Yin and Yang of Clothes

Walking into the Versace boutique, I feel relaxed and amused. I pass the glossy vinyl pants and dazzling striped tops, and pick up a scanty red shift decorated with three-inch metal zippers at the chest and longer zippers that serve as front pockets. The shift looks like a racy version of the housedresses my mother wore, except it's thirteen hundred dollars. I can imagine older women buying the cashmere sweaters in argyle pastels with gold lamé running through the wool, crowned with Medusa-head buttons. I notice the sharp stare of a saleswoman; I am an intruder with no intention to buy, and feel superior rejecting overdone, overpriced clothes.

In the Armani shop, I am tense looking at clothes that I find beautiful, racks of long beige jackets and slim-cut pants as delicately varied in shade as grains of sand, and gauzy blouses that move effortlessly, like a calm breeze. I feel out of place, self-conscious; I am among people with whom I don't belong, next to clothes that I cannot afford. His is a fairy-tale world of clothes, a kingdom that I could pretend to live in as a child, and still long for as an adult.

The styles of these two men were the yin and yang of my youth: clothes could make you look southern Italian or Anglo-Saxon, extravagant or refined, sexy or powerful. In choosing either style, I had something to lose. . . .

Weaving Myths in Fabric

"Who was he?" my mother asks me on the phone after reports about the Versace murder blare on CNN night after night. "Your brother said his clothes were *gavone*. Is that right?"

I avoided a direct answer, wanting to pay Versace homage with a small tribute, not a sarcastic quip. Afterward, I thought about what Versace had achieved with his look of elegant whimsy. I thought about the endurance of his media legend, how Versace, too, would be liked for what he was not, disliked for what he was not; how we all weave myths in fabric, create a self in the clothes we wear; how my impulse to reject his fanciful palette and Versace's desire to color his background had a similar beginning: the self-consciousness of a southern Italian past. So as I considered my mother's question, I realized that the man who wished to be a Medici was also due a peasant elegy. Yes, his clothes were *gavone*, and the world rightly proclaimed them chic.

Italian Americans Continue to Be Stereotyped in Popular Culture

George De Stefano

The dominant image of Italian Americans in contemporary American popular culture is that of the mobster and the *gavone*, a boorish and rude character, according to Italian American journalist George De Stefano. Despite the fact that the police in both the United States and Italy have seriously curbed organized crime, American television and film producers continue to create stories about Italian American criminals. The television program *The Sopranos* is a prime example, argues De Stefano, who writes frequently on cultural issues. In this excerpt from his article in the *Nation*, De Stefano describes the persistent stereotyping of Italian Americans in film and television as "infuriating" and discusses the many contributions Italian Americans have made to U.S. society.

The last decade of the twentieth century was not a happy one for the Mafia. During the nineties both the United States and Italy made remarkable strides in curbing organized crime, imprisoning gangsters and dismantling their business interests. Though it would be premature to declare either the Italian or the American Mafia dead, both have been wounded, the latter perhaps mortally. But if the

George De Stefano, "Ungood Fellas," *The Nation*, vol. 270, February 7, 2000, p. 31.
Copyright © 2000 by The Nation Company, LP. Reproduced by permission.

Mafia is a shadow of its former self, you'd hardly know it from pop culture. In fact, media images of La Cosa Nostra [Italian-dominated organized crime syndicate] seem to be proliferating in direct proportion to the decline of organized crime. Not since Francis Ford Coppola's *The Godfather* reinvented the gangster genre in the early seventies have there been so many wiseguys on screen. [1999] brought the films *Analyze This* and *Mickey Blue Eyes*, and with i fratelli [the brothers] Weinstein, Harvey and Bob, having acquired the rights to the late Mario Puzo's final novel, *Omerta*, for their Miramax Films, there's at least one other high-profile Mafia movie on the way. . . .

The Mafia on American Television

On television, gangsters with Italian surnames have been a surefire audience draw, from the days of *The Untouchables* to contemporary cop shows like *NYPD Blue*. A very partial list of recent programs includes the network miniseries *The Last Don* and *Bella Mafia*, as well as biopics about John Gotti and his turncoat lieutenant Sammy "The Bull" Gravano, and, on Showtime cable, an absurdly hagiographic one about Joseph Bonanno produced by his son, Bill. But no mob-themed show has generated the critical accolades and viewer enthusiasm accorded *The Sopranos*, the Emmy Award–winning HBO comedy-drama that has become the cable network's most-watched series. . . .

Moving from *The Sopranos'* suburban New Jersey turf to Palermo, HBO [in the fall of 1999] premiered *Excellent Cadavers*, a feature-film adaptation of Alexander Stille's 1995 book about the anti-Mafia campaign launched by two courageous Sicilian magistrates. Why is Italian-American (and Italian) organized crime such a mainstay of American pop culture, and do these images reflect the reality of the Mafia? And does the persistence of the Mafioso as a pop-culture archetype constitute ethnic defamation of Italian-Americans?

That many of today's depictions of the American Mafia are in the comic mode—*The Sopranos, Analyze This, Mickey Blue Eyes*, the parody *Mafia!*—is possible only because organized crime is much less fearsome than in its heyday. Both *The Sopranos* and *Analyze This* feature Mafiosi on the verge of a nervous breakdown, their psychological crackups reflecting the disarray of their criminal enterprises under the pressure of law enforcement and the breaking of omerta, the code of silence, by gangsters who'd rather sing than serve time. V. [Vittorio] Zucconi, a commentator for the Italian newspaper *La Repubblica*, analyzed this development in an article titled "America: The Decline of the Godfather." Zucconi claims that in the United States the Mafia survives mainly in its pop-culture representations, and that while it used to generate fear, today it is a source of humor. He says that in America one can observe "the funeral of the dying Mafia," an outcome he hopes one day will occur also in Italy. Is Zucconi overoptimistic?

Criminologist James Jacobs reaches a similar conclusion in his study *Gotham Unbound: How New York City was Liberated from the Clutches of Cosa Nostra* (NYU Press). Organized-crime-control strategies "have achieved significant success in purging Cosa Nostra from the city's social, economic, and political life," he writes. Gangsters in New York, and also in other large and small cities, are losing their foothold in the labor and industrial rackets that have been the source of their power and influence; and there is a dearth of younger, rising stars to replace aging or incarcerated leaders. The decline, says Jacobs, has been so marked that "Cosa Nostra's survival into the next millennium . . . can be seriously doubted." It's a different story in Italy. The Sicilian Mafia's economic might, its alliances with politicians and indifferent law enforcement enabled it to grow so powerful that it threatened Italy's status as a modern nation. As Alexander Stille observed in

Excellent Cadavers, the war against the Mafia in Sicily is not a local problem of law and order but the struggle for national unity and democracy in Italy. HBO's film based on Stille's book promised to tell that story, but, at barely ninety minutes, it ended up too compressed to offer more than a skim on the events he reported and analyzed so compellingly. Talk about missed opportunities: Instead of the Z-like political thriller[1] it could have been, *Cadavers* is a rather routine policier. . . .

The Italian-American Response

Italians overwhelmingly regard Mafiosi as the other; they do not identify or empathize with criminals, nor do they feel that portrayals of organized crime in movies, television and other media tar them with the brush of criminality. Many Italian-Americans, however, regard the seemingly endless stream of Mafia movies and TV shows as a defamatory assault. In mid-January [2000] a coalition of seven Italian-American organizations issued a joint statement condemning *The Sopranos* for "defaming and assassinating the cultural character" of Americans of Italian descent.

It's undeniable that the dominant pop-culture images of Italian-Americans have been the mobster and the related, anti-working class stereotype of the boorish *gavone* [rude, ignorant, low-class person]. But there are important differences between these skewed portrayals and other forms of ethnic stereotyping. If the Mafia has been conflated with Sicilian/Italian culture, it's in large part because Italian-American filmmakers and writers have so expertly blended the two. Coppola's memorable and authentic depiction of an Italian-American wedding in *The Godfather* comes to mind. *The Sopranos*, created by veteran TV writer David Chase (ne De Cesare), similarly gets

1. a film based on a true story of a cop who went after corrupt politicians

many details right about nouveau riche suburban Italian-Americans, the eponymous mob family's noncriminal neighbors.

The Sopranos cleverly acknowledges Italian-American indignation over Mafia stereotyping only to try to co-opt it. In an episode from the show's first season, Dr. Jennifer Melfi, Tony Soprano's psychiatrist, and her family have a lively dinnertime debate about the persistence of the mob image. The scene ends with the Melfis toasting the "20 million Italian Americans" who have nothing to do with organized crime. But Jennifer also mocks her ex-husband, an ethnic activist, for being more concerned about "rehabilitating Connie Francis's reputation" than with ethnic cleansing. The line neatly skewers the tunnel vision of conservative Italian-Americans who ignore forms of bias and social injustice that don't affect them. But it also poses a false dichotomy: caring passionately about the image of one's group need not preclude a broader perspective. At other times, the show suggests that Tony, a murderous criminal, is an Italian-American everyman. He's aware of his people's history—he informs his daughter that the telephone was invented not by Alexander Graham Bell but by Antonio Meucci—and he's depicted as more honest and vital than his snooty neighbors, or, as he calls them, the "Wonder-Bread wops."

Pop Culture and Italian Ethnicity

The Mafia has become the paradigmatic pop-culture expression of Italian-American ethnicity for several reasons: the aura of glamour, sometimes tragic, surrounding the movie mobster, exemplified by Coppola's Corleones; the gangster genre's embodiment of the violent half of "kiss kiss, bang bang," [Film critic] Pauline Kael's famous distillation of the essential preoccupations of American movies; and, perhaps most important, the enduring appeal of the outlaw—the guy who, in a technocratic, impersonal society, has the personal power to reward friends, and, more important, whack enemies. Although real Mafiosi are venal and violent, films and TV too often have presented them far more sympathetically than they deserve—*The Sopranos* is just the latest case in point.

Italian-Americans, whose forebears fled *la miseria*, the crushing poverty of southern Italy and Sicily, in numbers so vast that their departure has been likened to a hemorrhage, constitute one of the United States' largest ethnic groups. An Italian-American film critic and author told me some years ago that it was "selfish" of our *paesani* [countrymen] to complain about Mafia stereotyping given their largely successful pursuit of the American Dream and the more onerous discrimination faced by other minorities. He also insisted that most Americans are smart enough to realize that gangsters constitute only a tiny minority of the Italian-American population.

But it is dismaying—no, infuriating—to see one's group depicted so consistently in such distorted fashion. Unlike racist stereotyping of blacks, portrayals of Italian-American criminality don't reflect or reinforce Italian-American exclusion from American society and its opportunities. (Faced with a threatened NAACP boycott, both the NBC and ABC networks recently agreed to increase the hiring of blacks, Latinos and Asians, in front of and behind the TV cameras.) The pervasiveness of these images, however, does affect the perception of Italian-Americans by others. Surveys indicate that many Americans believe that most Italian-Americans are in some way "connected" and that Italian immigrants created organized crime in the United States, even though the Irish, Germans and others got there first.

Besides fostering such attitudes, the Mafia mystique also serves to obscure other, more interesting and no less dramatic aspects of the Italian-American experience. In 1997 the City University of New York hosted a conference on "The Lost World of Italian American Radicalism." Scholars discussed the immigrant anarchists [Nicola] Sacco and [Bartolomeo] Vanzetti (executed by the US government), other major figures like the labor organizer Carlo Tresca, the New York City Congressman Vito Marcantonio and such icons of sixties activism as civil rights advocate Father James Groppi and Mario Savio of the Berkeley Free Speech movement. The conference also highlighted unsung men and women who were labor militants, anti-Fascist organizers and politically engaged writers and artists.

Besides such efforts to recover and understand the radical past, there has been a surge of cultural production and activism among Italian-Americans. In recent years the American-Italian Historical Association, a national organization of academics and grassroots scholars, has held conferences on such hot-button topics as multiculturalism and race relations. Fieri, an association of young Italian-American professionals, . . . commemorated the life and work of Vito Marcantonio—an amazing choice given the far less controversial figures they could have honored. The New York–based Italian-American Writers Association and journals such as *Voices in Italian Americana* (VIA) and *The Italian American Review* promote and publish fiction, poetry and critical essays by writers whose vision of italianita flouts the pop-culture cliches. Italo-American gays and lesbians have come out with *Hey, Paisan!*, a new anthology, and *Fuori!*, a folio of essays published by VIA. Actor/playwright Frank Ingrasciotta's *Blood Type: Ragu*, . . . enjoying a successful run at the Belmont Italian American Theater in the Bronx (several of whose productions have moved to Off Broadway), offers an exploration of Sicilian-American identity and culture free of goombahs with guns.

Ethnicity remains a powerful and contentious force in American life, and popular culture should illumine its workings. Italian-Americans who want to promote more diverse depictions might not only protest Hollywood film studios and TV production companies. They might put some of the onus on Italian-American creative talents who have built careers on the Mafia. And they could also support the alternative, community-level work being done. Other stories from Italo-America can and should be told.

Italian Immigrants' Feelings of Shame

Roland Merullo

In the next selection Roland Merullo explores the self-hatred and shame that afflict many racial and ethnic groups in the United States, including Italian Americans. He describes his Italian grandparents as examples of immigrants who came to America determined to succeed and to create a better life for their children. However, in their drive to "fit in better," the family gave up much of its cultural heritage. Faced with widespread discrimination and poverty, they developed a sense of shame about their Italian origins and did not teach their children the Italian language. Merullo, a writer who has taught at Bennington and Amherst colleges, says the problem of shame and self-hatred is compounded by stereotypes regarding Italian Americans in the popular culture—in particular, their portrayal as criminals and Mafia members. Merullo vows to reclaim his ethnic identity, to embrace more of his Italian heritage, and to resist those stereotypes that falsely define him.

My own parents were the children of immigrants—southern Italians on my father's side, and poor English Catholics on my mother's—and it is easy enough to trace the fine thread of shame and self-consciousness that runs through me, my parents, my grandparents, and back to the bigotry they endured when they first came to this country. That does not mean we stumble through the world hanging our heads, apologizing, and feeling badly about ourselves. Nei-

Roland Merullo, "Hatred and Its Sly Legacy," *Chronicle of Higher Education*, vol. 47, December 1, 2000, p. B10. Copyright © 2000 by *Chronicle of Higher Education*. Reproduced by permission of the author.

ther does it mean that we blame our individual failings on enemies from long ago. What it means is that old insults have mutated within us, forming small pockets of awkwardness, bloated pride, self-consciousness, and buried anger.

It seems to me that one of the best examples of this hatred-shame connection is the fact that my father's parents—who came to America near the turn of the last century—did not bring up their eight children in a bilingual household. Though, as boys and girls, they heard the language spoken in their home, my surviving aunts and uncles on that side of the family remember only a few dozen phrases of Italian. When asked why, they answer with some regret that their mother and father emphasized English because they wanted their children to "fit in better" with the America that surrounded them.

The Drive Toward Assimilation

On the one hand, that drive toward assimilation seems a natural, even an admirable response to life in the New World, given the environment of the day. Having left behind the perils and privations of the southern Italian countryside (a place, in 1900, where upward mobility was the stuff of the afterlife), my grandparents did not want to handicap their American-born children by making them seem in any way foreign. In comparison with what they had known in their Campanian villages, this country was a vast garden of opportunity: Why hobble their offspring in the corner where only tomatoes and basil grew? Why make them Different, when the road to success was paved with Same?

On the other hand, it seems clear to me now that their motivations weren't so purely pragmatic, that a measure of shame was involved. In a more welcoming environment, they would have encouraged their children to speak both languages, but being Italian in America in the first half of the 20th century meant experiencing ubiquitous mockery, poverty, widespread and unchallenged discrimination, and difficulty in finding good work. . . .

The Damaged Self

I grew up in a largely Italian-American enclave just outside Boston proper, a place that puts its own twists on the local accent. When I listen to my adult voice on tape—even now, 25 years after having left that neighborhood—I am surprised to hear, not "dese" and "dose" exactly, but a certain slight hardening of the "th" sound. It is something I could change, just as I probably could change my Boston accent, but the more purely American speech, the speech of the academy, would feel awkward on my tongue. Phony, as we used to say in the old neighborhood, where inauthenticity was second only to disloyalty on the list of cardinal sins.

A small thing, perhaps. No doubt I am more sensitive to my hard t-h's than most listeners, in the faculty lounge or elsewhere. But that heightened self-consciousness, that faint expectation of mockery, is precisely the point. My sensitivity has to do with not wanting to give credence to the old criticisms that were leveled against Americans of my ancestry—that they were crude, loud, violent, insufficiently intellectual, and overly emotional.

In people from other ethnic backgrounds, that self-consciousness takes different forms. I had African-American friends in college, and met others, later, in the academy, who were so determined never to make themselves vulnerable to racist criticisms that they developed an excessively careful manner of speaking and behaving. In effect, they traded their "African-ness," a piece of their identity, for acceptance, just as so many other groups in the melting pot have done. Some of that is a necessary and healthy compromise—in one way or another, all of us trim our sails in order to travel with the fleet. And who is to say precisely what "African-ness" is? Like Italian-ness, it can take many forms. But, in the case of those friends at least, it seemed to me that the price of "fitting in better" was a damaged self. They had traded away too much of their authenticity and individuality—distorted their speech patterns, lost or hid their ebullience, passion, and empathy.

Clichés About Italian-Americans

One Italian-American professor I know swears that his fellow teachers scrutinize him for signs of latent violent tendencies, as if anyone with black hair and a name that ends in a vowel must have a darker side straight out of *The Godfather* or *The Sopranos*. I believe him. Even now, I occasionally feel the shadow of such clichés—reaffirmed constantly by popular culture—falling over me in the classroom, in job interviews, in pricey hotels or restaurants. How peculiar it is that Hollywood, radio, and television continue to pump fresh juice into those stereotypes, long after the media have been made hype-conscious of characterizations that may be offensive to just about every other group.

One example: A few years ago, Garrison Keillor had a talented young mimic as a guest on his "Prairie Home Companion" radio show. The girl had a real genius for making different voices come out of her mouth, and performed a variety of skits that highlighted her ability. I was enjoying the broadcast until I heard her say, in a threatening, gravelly voice: "Blow da safe, Rocco."

Rocco?

A gentle, approving laughter rippled through the audience. Would the reaction have been the same if she'd said, "Eat the watermelon, Tyrone," or "Don't pinch that penny, Jacob," or "Please ask Maria to stop eating tortillas and start doing some work"?

Italian-American professors find themselves in the odd predicament of presiding over classrooms in which they can feel the politically correct antennae trembling in the air—yet that correctness does not quite extend to their own tender spots. In a novel-writing class I taught recently, a class in which we used *The Great Gatsby* as a text, a Jewish student noted, with some pain in her voice, that "the bad guy [Wolfsheim] is a Jew."

"I know how you feel," I blurted out. "What do you think it's like for me that four out of every five leg-breakers in books and movies are named Bruno, Vito, or Guido?"

Perhaps I should have been more restrained, stifled my own sensitivities in the name of maintaining some idealized professorial persona. But that ideal grew out of a dominant culture that was Anglo-Saxon and white, and I share only one of those labels. Or perhaps, here and in the classroom, I should acknowledge that Jews and blacks have suffered so much more from bigotry than Italians ever did, and that, since Italians have blended so well into all aspects of American life, the words "guinea" and "wop" soon will fade from the American vocabulary entirely, or at least become as taboo as other ugly emblems of hatred, such as "nigger," "spic," and "kike." But the question is not who has suffered more, and who has more right to complain about it. The question is a modern version of the same one my grandparents faced: How do we balance the blending with the preserving? How can we be American and "professional" without blotting out the rest of who we are—our womanliness, our blackness, our Italian-ness? The real question is: What is lost to academic culture when descendants of the victims of hatred are shamed into subverting aspects of themselves that the dominant culture derides?

Reclaiming Authenticity

In struggling to answer that question, I have come to believe it is both good for me and good for the academy that I put a hand on students' shoulders when I am talking to them—when it seems right for me to do that—because, in my corner of the American garden, that gesture was neither sexual nor a matter of power, but implied commiseration, affection, and respect. After years of trying to be reserved, I now believe it is perfectly fine to express emotion in the classroom if I am moved by a story or a stanza of poetry: To me, that emotion is part and parcel of the value of literature. To talk with my hands, to keep my speech patterns the way they are as long as they fall within the general laws of standard grammar, to be the person I actually am—an American from a working-class, primarily Italian background—those qualities give me authenticity, and help give the stew its spice.

I do not walk into the classroom or the cafeteria wearing a red, white, and green arm band proclaiming my portion of Italian blood, making a fuss about my ethnicity and showing off old scars and bruises at the smallest sign of insult. The American academy has enough of that behavior to go around, and much of it seems like self-indulgent narcissism rather than concern for fairness.

But neither do I let myself be governed by the echoes—quieter now—of old catcalls, and lace my cultural inheritance, an inheritance I happen to like, into a tight suit that goes by the name "professionalism" and seems somehow less than human to me. To teach within the constraints of that tight girdle would mean accepting defeat at the hands of the bigots of the last century. It would mean carrying into the classroom or the faculty lounge a person I am not. How could such a person—such a phony, my aunts and uncles might say—be of any benefit to a student, an institution, or the academy as a whole? How can anyone who is crippled by shame—Italian-American, African-American, Mexican-American, homosexual, or female—show any love for students or colleagues? And, without the balm of love, how can the wounds of hatred ever heal?

CHAPTER 4

Profiles of Famous
Italian Americans

COMING TO AMERICA

Martin Scorsese: Film Director

Martin Scorsese, as told to Mary Pat Kelly

Martin Scorsese is one of America's most respected film-makers. He was born and grew up in New York City in an Italian American family where the Sicilian dialect was spoken at home. As a teen Scorsese planned to become a Catholic priest but he was expelled from the seminary for unruly behavior. He graduated from New York University and began making films in the 1960s. Over the years, his films have won many awards and Academy Award nominations. He also has received a lifetime achievement award from the American Film Institute. Many of his films, including *Taxi Driver, Raging Bull,* and *GoodFellas,* have been critically acclaimed; other films such as *The Last Temptation of Christ* have been more controversial. His work often includes religious themes and graphic violence. In 1974 Scorsese made a documentary film, *Italianamerican,* about his parents, Charles and Catherine Scorsese. In this interview with Mary Pat Kelly about the making of *Italianamerican,* Scorsese discusses this film, his childhood desire to become a priest, growing up in a rough New York City neighborhood, and his lifelong love of the movies. Mary Pat Kelly is a filmmaker and author. Her works include *Martin Scorsese: That First Decade* and *Martin Scorsese: A Journey,* from which the following selection is extracted.

The movie *Italianamerican,* a film I made about my parents in 1974, is, I think, the best film I ever made. It really

Mary Pat Kelly, *Martin Scorsese: A Journey*. New York: Thunder's Mouth Press, 1991. Copyright © 1991 by Mary Pat Kelly. All rights reserved. Appears by permission of the publisher, Thunder's Mouth Press, a division of Avalon Publishing Group.

freed me in style. I was able to shoot this footage, in 16 millimeter, of my parents in their apartment on the Lower East Side [New York City]. We were having dinner on a Saturday and a Sunday and I shot it in six hours. My friends made up some questions about immigration, about how the family came over, because it was made as part of a series called "Storm of Strangers" for the National Endowment for the Humanities for the bicentennial of 1976. It had to be twenty-eight minutes long, they said. One was on the Irish, one on the Jews, Chinese, Polish, etc. They asked me to do the Italians. I said no. But finally I said, "Yes, I will, if we don't do it the way that you normally see. I don't want to go back to 1901 with stock footage and a narrator saying, 'In 1901 . . .'" But I did wind up taking some of the footage from the archives; it is really interesting. I said, "Let's ask my parents these questions." My parents worked in the garment district all their lives. They stick to the emotions. That's what I wanted to hear, some emotion.

My mother talks a great deal, and my father is quite reticent, usually. He sat on one side of the big couch in the living room and my mother sat on the other side. The camera panned over. And she said, "Well, what do you want me to say?" I said, "Well, just, you know, talk." There were no questions. So she looks at my father and says, "Why are you sitting over there?" Then I *knew*. I said, "This is going to be easier than I thought. In fact, I'm going to lose control of the thing if I don't watch out." It's a whole other thing up there with your parents, trying to control them. It's quite extraordinary and I felt it came out in the film. . . .

I get my timing from my mother. She is a great storyteller, humorous, emotional. My father tells good stories too, but his are more somber. She has the emotion. But the structure is not straightforward. Even now I get interested in the emotion of a shot and sometimes forget to give the audience the plot information they need.

Italianamerican tells a series of stories. But because of the structuring of the questions and their answers, a bigger story came out overall. And that was a work-in-progress. It was terrific. It was fun. It was learning. We shot medium shots of people talking, and intercut with some music over stills of them. To me it seemed very, very strong. It smashed all those preconceptions about what a film should look like and how a film should be presented. It also freed me, in a sense. It streamlined the style for *Taxi Driver*. And in *Raging Bull*, we didn't give a damn. We didn't care about transitions, really. What I should say is, we didn't care about *artful* transitions.

In certain parts of *Italianamerican* mother is talking, and we put in twenty frames of black. Then we cut back and she's taking another breath, and she keeps going. It looks like the film was off for a second. Who cares? It doesn't matter. I said, "This is amazing.". . .

Scorsese's Italian Neighborhood

When the Sicilians came over to New York, the first ones must have settled on Elizabeth Street. Then they wrote to their friends in Sicily, "Come over, we've got rooms for you." And they all settled there, on Elizabeth Street. The Neapolitans, somehow, wound up on Mulberry. Each group wanted to be together. So they kept telling their friends, "We've got rooms for you here." The Sicilians brought with them a village culture. A medieval culture or older, based around dukes. The dukes were the *capos* [head] of each village. The *capo* took the place of the government in Sicily. There was no such things as police. I mean, how could you trust them? After two thousand years, four thousand years of being the penal colony of the world, how could a Sicilian trust the authorities?

There was no such thing as law. It was a feudal system. And they did the same in New York. Village to village. And so you had the man, the *capo*, who would preside over family disagreements—sit down, have a cup of coffee with them, and say, "Now you can't fight like this. It's very bad for the rest of the family. You've got to come together." At the same time, he may have been a killer, too. We don't know. I can't say that. But they were the law in many different respects.

My parents went from Elizabeth Street to Queens, where I was born. But when I was seven I had to survive this major trauma: We moved from Corona, where there were at least a few trees, back to the Lower East Side. . . .

Scorsese's Childhood

During the first five or six years of my life, I was mainly in the movie theater. I had asthma as a child and was not able to participate in children's games or sports of any kind, so my parents took me to the movies. My brother did too. It became a place to dream, fantasize, to feel at home. . . .

I became enamored of the church when I was seven. We had Italian priests and Irish nuns. I went to Catholic school and the nuns taught us that this terrific thing happens; at 10:30 every morning God comes down to the altar, and it's great. Also, I had to survive, so religion became a kind of way of survival, too. I tried to understand what the priests were talking about, and deal with that, and after a while, *be* like that—be like a priest, especially the young priests.

My feeling about God was a good feeling. Of course, there were always, fears, like, if you see the face of God you're going to die, or the story about the man who tried to save the Ark of the Covenant and touched it, and died on the spot. We always had those fears as kids. But the sense of God was loving and great, really wonderful. Especially Jesus, the incarnation. What he did. I became an altar boy because I loved the ritual, the chance to be close to that special moment when God came down to the altar.

For me, Holy Week was always a very powerful time, even more dramatic than Christmas. The rituals were dramatic. The liturgies were beautiful. The Stations of the Cross were very dramatic. This colored my whole sense of God. I preferred Christmas, as I guess everyone does, because you get gifts, and it's more fun. It's a happy time. But in Holy Week, you have to go through Spy Wednesday, Holy Thursday, Good Friday, and Holy Saturday to reach Easter Sunday. The names alone are dramatic. It's called Passion Week. It's very terrifying. It's a scary time. But it's exhilarating, too, and very beautiful.

A young priest in our parish, Father Principe, was a strong influence on me. Not that everything he liked I liked. For example, he was into the serious films, Fred Zimmermann films and that sort of thing.

I remember the first time Father Principe came to make a speech when I was in sixth grade. It was after one of the Academy Award presentations. He said, "Were all of you kids watching the Academy Awards last night?" We said, "Yes, Father." He then made the analogy between the statuette and a false God—greed, money, and fame!

Of course, he was young, he was only about twenty-five. But he was right about the greed, this concept of me, me, me, and getting up there and getting that award, and feeling, "Now I'm better than . . ." I'll always remember that. "Look at that!" he said. "It looks like the idol Moloch!" Remember Cecil B. De Mille's *Samson and Delilah?*

I remember talking to him about Hitchcock's *I Confess.* He was a young priest, and had to deal with celibacy. "Listen," he said. "This film is just outrageous." He said you can't have a premise of a film where a man becomes a priest because he is, in a sense, jilted in a love affair by Anne Baxter. It's crazy. He said, "The priesthood is demanding. If that's the reason you go in, you'll never make it. You'll never stay. A few months, maybe a year, but after a year . . ." And that's, you know, that's the truth.

And I'll never forget the day I saw *Pal Joey*. I was at the Capitol Theatre with Joe Moralli. We came back on Mulberry Street and said, "Father, we've seen the greatest picture with Frank Sinatra. He plays this dancer and he's such a bum, and has all these girls, but he's such a wonderful character." He said, "What is it with you boys? What's the matter with you? A beautiful day like today, and you're in the movie theater again? You should play basketball!"

I talked to him about a lot of things. Especially after I decided to be a priest. I was very taken by religion. I was also taken by the great story of Jesus and his love. That to me is the most important part of it. The theatricality that went with it was extraordinary, of course, but to me, it was about this incredible character, and about those events.

However, to take a religion like that seriously, and then hit those streets that are full of lawlessness, is another story. You want to know how to combine it and try to put the two together. It's impossible. And this is really just a microcosm of the world, isn't it? . . .

I was quite serious about the priesthood and I went to the minor seminary of the Archdiocese of New York for a year. I planned to enter an order of priests after I graduated from Cardinal Hayes High School.

I grew up with a lot of tough guys. They took care of me, and later, after they died, I found out that they were monsters—bloodsuckers, horrible! But they were very sweet to me. I don't go down to the old neighborhood to see them anymore. I was raised with them, the gangsters and the priests. That's it. Nothing in between. I wanted to be a cleric. I guess the passion I had for religion wound up mixed with film, and now, as an artist, in a way, I'm both gangster and priest.

Geraldine Ferraro: Legislator and Vice Presidential Candidate

Geraldine Ferraro

After graduating from Marymount Manhattan College in 1956, Geraldine Ferraro worked during the day as a teacher and attended Fordham University Law School at night, graduating in 1960. Ferraro entered public life in 1974 as an assistant district attorney in New York City. She was elected to the U.S. Congress in 1978 and served three terms before she was selected by Democratic Party presidential candidate Walter Mondale to be his running mate in the 1984 presidential election. She was the first woman to run for vice president of the United States. Ferraro's educational and political achievements did not come easily. In this excerpt from her book, *Framing a Life*, Ferraro pays tribute to the women who have been her role models, especially her mother Antonetta Ferraro. Geraldine Ferraro's Italian immigrant father Dominick Ferraro died when Geraldine was eight, leaving Antonetta to support the family. Ferraro describes how her mother and grandmother before her struggled against the obstacles facing immigrants and the Italian cultural limitations on women and how they nurtured her achievements.

My mother, Antonetta Ferraro, was a crochet beader. From the time she was fourteen, her fingers were busy, working deftly, her body bent forward over the large wooden bead-

Geraldine Ferraro, with Catherine Whitney, *Framing a Life: A Family Memoir*. New York: A Lisa Drew Book, Scribner, 1998. Copyright © 1998 by Geraldine A. Ferraro. All rights reserved. Reproduced by permission of Scribner, an imprint of Simon & Schuster Adult Publishing Group.

ing frame. She crocheted spangles and imitation pearls, glittering pieces of glass, onto the satins, silks, and chiffons worn to weddings, galas, and balls.

She had no glitter in her life, but Antonetta did have a design in her head—a design that imitated the success stories of other immigrant families. She understood the value of education, not just for my brother, Carl, but for me, the daughter, the girl. She fashioned my life, my future, in the same way she worked the fabrics—carefully, with a skillful eye.

My nomination to the second-highest office in the land was her proudest moment. When I stood in front of the delegates and spoke about my immigrant heritage, I was overcome by the feeling that this moment belonged to her and to her mother more than it belonged to me. I remember how much I wanted to reach out with every word and hand them a return on their investment.

I knew in my heart that I would not be standing on that stage had my grandmother Maria Giuseppa Caputo not stood in steerage with her maiden aunt on the SS *Italia* and crossed to America in 1890. I would not have had the resources to run for Congress in 1978 if my mother, Antonetta Ferraro, hadn't impressed upon me the value of education, a privilege she herself was denied. Like countless others from my generation, I reaped the benefits of the sacrifices and hard labor of my immigrant legacy. I was the beneficiary of my mother's dreams—the ones she could not keep for herself but saved for me as a remarkable trousseau.

It occurs to me that the pioneers are never themselves heralded as heroes. They clear the path so that others may make a safe journey to their destination. Yet it is they who take the risks, who suffer to advance their dreams. By the time I had achieved the full potential of the American dream, it was no longer unthinkable that a woman could sit in Congress, become vice president or even president. Others had fought the worst battles before me. I stood on their backs to reach the gold ring. By the time my own two daughters embarked on their careers, in business and in medicine, the paths to their goals were already well worn.

Ferraro's Role Models

It took me most of my lifetime to understand that my grandmother and my mother were my true role models. It wasn't readily apparent. My grandmother was Italian, bound by language and tradition to a world I never knew. My mother was a first-generation Italian American, straddling the past and the future—serving as a bridge between the two worlds. She could speak to her mother in her language and to me in mine. But I was all American, a modern woman, impatient with the past. My focus was on the future. I was eager to break free of the restrictions that women like my grandmother and mother experienced. I deemed these limitations intolerable. My grandmother and mother had been raised in eras when education and independence were not considered, or even desirable, for women. Dominated by strong men, they fell naturally into supporting roles. Constrained as they were by the daily task of caring for others, their identities did not belong to them but to their husbands, their children, and to large extended families with never-ending needs.

They were also controlled by the most powerful force of all—a set of cultural customs and mandates that belonged to another world, across the ocean, but had planted itself firmly in the tight-knit immigrant communities of America. From the time I was a young girl, I carried the warning in my head, stated over and over again: Don't step outside the lines. People will talk. (It was considered the worst thing in the world for people to talk!) Women's lives were consumed by invisible but very real boundaries. That is why my grandmother, a beautiful, high-spirited girl of fifteen, did not object to marrying a man nearly old enough to be her father—a widower with a child. The maiden aunt she had accompanied to America died soon after their arrival, and my grandmother's options disappeared. Her future was arranged for her by others, and she accepted her plight. She became a child bride and stepmother and went on to bear nine children of her own.

Cultural expectations controlled my mother's fate as well. Although she was bright and she desperately loved school, she hid her disappointment when her mother made her quit at age fourteen and sent her to work in the garment district because the family needed her paycheck.

When I was young, I recognized and appreciated the sacrifices of my mother and grandmother, but I felt certain that these were not models I ever wanted to follow. From my earliest memory I knew I could do whatever I wanted to do. I lived in a world without limits. I was the first female in my family to go to college, and I attended with Irish, German, and Polish girls who were the first in theirs as well. We didn't have much money, but we were not restricted by the times or by our ethnic backgrounds.

The Andretti Family: Race Car Champions

Ed Hinton

Mario Andretti is known around the world for his long and successful career as a top race car driver in such events as the Indianapolis 500, the United States Auto Club (USAC) circuit races, and Formula One races. Mario is the most famous member of a racing dynasty—the Andretti family—that includes Mario's brother Aldo (whose career was cut short by two serious accidents), Mario's sons Michael and Jeff, and Aldo's son John. In the following excerpt from a *Sports Illustrated* article by journalist Ed Hinton, Mario and his mother talk about the family's origins in northern Italy, how the family became refugees when their village was annexed by Yugoslavia, the family's immigration to the United States, and Mario and Aldo's early entrance into the racing life.

Before the slavic partisans came, fighting the Germans and the troops of Il Duce [Fascist Italian dictator Benito Mussolini], Montona was a village of carts and donkeys and horses. "Even after the war start, we have only one—what you call?—taxi," says Nonna Rina [the Andretti twins' mother] in English broken but lovely. The cobblestones were scrubbed and polished by hand, the town traffic-free, so there was no clear inspiration for the vocal sounds her twin sons began to make in the summer of 1942.

"When they were two, they begin to run," Nonna Rina

Ed Hinton, "Inherit the Wind: The Andretti Family," *Sports Illustrated*, May 11, 1992, pp. 78–93. Copyright © 1992 by *Sports Illustrated*. Reproduced by permission.

says. "They were going into the cabinet in the kitchen and taking the lids from the pots and running around the table [she gestures as if with a steering wheel], saying, '*Roooom, roooom*.' And when they are going to sleep, they are pretending they are little cars. Into the pillowcase they are saying, '*Roooom, roooom*,' until I was yelling at them: '*Va a dormire!*'

"'Go to sleep!' I said. Still, *roooom, roooom. Sì.*"

Where did they get such notions? Nonna Rina, who is now 79, throws up her hands, "I think they have on their blood."

Son Mario

One of her twins, Mario Andretti—the most famous racing driver in the world and, at 52 [in 1992] head of the most famous and prolific racing family ever—stares out across his backyard pool at dusk in Nazareth, Pa. His gaze is across the Atlantic, and across the years. "It seems so remote from today," he says. "Like a life that didn't happen almost."

On a table beside him is a book about his beloved Istrian Peninsula. Once a gleaming finger of northeastern Italy jutting into the Adriatic, once a sanctuary of Roman architecture unspoiled other than by millennia of gentle rain, it is now just another province of the devastated country that was Yugoslavia.

Nonna Rina—"Grandma Rina" to the new generation of Andretti drivers, Mario's two sons and his nephew—refers to the region as "this Istria," as if she has adapted Shakespeare's exaltation over England: *This blessed plot, this earth, this realm, this Istria.* And on this Istria basked Montona, about 25 miles from Trieste. "The town was so beautiful," says Mario. "In the '40s, when we still lived there, everything was so spick-and-span. All the hardware on the doorways was polished. The cobblestones were all polished. It's not like that now."

It is not even Montona now. For more than 40 years it has been called Motovun, Croatia. And in that time the very name Andretti has become virtually synonymous with motor racing. A poll taken in 1989 revealed the name Andretti to be as well known in the U.S. as (A.J.) Foyt and (Richard) Petty *together*. And of all the drivers in the world, only Mario Andretti, from experience, knows this: One cannot fathom fame by merely winning the Indianapolis 500 and the Daytona 500, which he has done. One must also win the world driving championship of Formula One, and then, he says, "walk into some drugstore in some obscure section of Paris or Madrid or São Paulo. . . ."

Mario gazes into the gathering dusk of the day, across the pool and across the Atlantic. "What a chain of events," he says. "*What* a chain of events.". . .

The Andrettis Become Refugees

"Before, in this Istria," says Nonna Rina, "we were very—how you say?—in good shape. Pretty rich. Because we have a lot of land . . . and we have the winery."

And then nothing. Her eyes dance and mist at the same time as she remembers the last of the good times in this Istria.

"Was wartime. There were no toys. Nothing to eat, either. So when Mario and Aldo are five, my mother's brother build them this little car, made of wood." She describes something along the lines of a soapbox-derby car. "The wheels are going fast, very fast. Montona is on a hill, and all the streets were like this." Her hands sweep downward. "And we have a street coming where all the benches and the people were sitting—oh, yes, a *park*—and this is their 'track.'"

And now her voice grows progressively higher and more gleeful. "One time, one lady she was coming up from the street, up the hill, and she see them coming, and she was yelling. 'Oh! My God!' because she thought they would be killed. They said. 'Go 'way! Go 'way! Let us run, 'cause we know where we have to go! We no wanna kill you!'"

Nothing could stop the little car from tearing down the streets. Not even the soldiers who came to the streets of Montona, or the partisans who fought them.

"And then they fight for 40 days, and the Communists take over," says Nonna Rina. "After the war the Communists take all this peninsula, this Istria. They take everything from you, and they no can pay with the money, but with the coupon. And until 1948 we have to live under Communist regime. . . .

"Every night somebody disappear. They were coming,

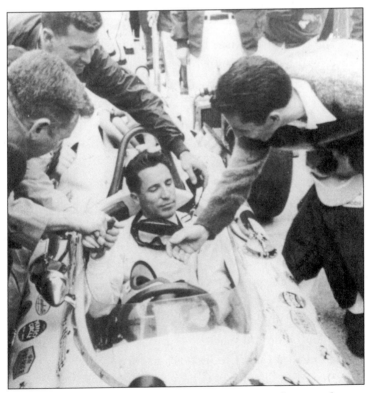

Mario Andretti's fascination with auto racing began when he was still a young boy living in Italy.

knock the door; you can talk nothing, because you was afraid. And they were killing all these young people coming home from the army.

"My brother, he was the one who have a motorcycle," says Nonna Rina. "And he race, and oh, he drive my mother crazy!" But when the Andretti twins were toddlers, their uncle was living elsewhere. So his exploits could not have directly sparked their "roooom, roooom"—it could only have been "on their blood."

The family Andretti has often discussed the possible reasons why they were not killed by the Communists in Istria. Aldo has a theory. "At one point the whole town of Montona, about 3,500 people, had worked for my father," he says. "They got all the worst people of Montona to join the Communist party and gave them power. But they never had the nerve to abuse this power against my father, because he'd fed all those people at one time or another. We like to think that's the reason they spared our family."

"In 1948," says Nonna Rina, "they decided to give the Italian people the option to leave this peninsula and go to the motherland, Italy. Three hundred and fifty thousand people, they left this Istria, 1948."

Gigi and Rina Andretti and their children (Aldo and Mario were eight by then, and Annamaria was 14 [their sister]) were sent to a refugee camp in Lucca, Italy, about 45 miles from Florence. "And we were there," says Nonna Rina, "for seven years and a half." In Lucca the twins' love of racing billowed into a consuming passion. In the family's one room—actually a space defined by blankets hung to separate the Andrettis from other refugee families—Mario and Aldo hid magazines and sporting papers telling of Grand Prix racing in its postwar form, which was newly designated as "Formula One."

"Every time the old man would see us with the magazines, he always would say, 'Crazy kids!'" says Mario. . . .

Coming to America

Then, says Aldo, came "quite a jolt." Nonna Rina had an uncle who had emigrated to Nazareth, Pa., and he offered to bring one family, that of Nonna Rina's brother, over to America. But, says Nonna Rina, "my sister-in-law, she don't want to leave her parents, and she say she don't want to come in this country. And so I have the opportunity for my family.

"Really, I didn't want to come in this country because I don't like to leave my parents and all my relatives there, but I was forced, because I have three children, and we have to think for their future."

The twins were sick at the thought. "As kids, we had all our dreams in place," says Mario. "And all of a sudden we're displacing to a new world, where we only knew of one race happening—Indianapolis. And so it didn't seem like we were going to be able to fulfill our dreams. But in fact it was probably just the opposite. We probably never would have fulfilled our dreams if we had stayed there."

At just after 6 A.M. on the morning of June 16, 1955, the Italian ocean liner *Conte Biancamano* steamed past the Statue of Liberty and into New York Harbor.

"I can see my children now," Nonna Rina says, beaming. "They were so happy. You could see in their faces. And they were singing."

That is not how Mario and Aldo recall it. They whispered to each other, "No *corse* in America." No racing in America. The five Andrettis joined their American relatives in Nazareth, 70 miles from New York. The twins seemed destined to a secure but uninspiring future of steel mills or desk jobs.

Three days later Aldo was lying in his bed with a migraine headache when Mario came thundering up the stairs of their great-uncle's house, shouting, "*Eh, Aldo! Nazareth ha und pista per le corse!*" ["Hey, Aldo! Nazareth has a racetrack!"]

Aldo sprang from the bed, forgetting his headache. Nazareth had a racetrack. And so the Andretti twins saw for the first time the strangest *pista* they had ever encountered, an oval track with a dirt surface, not at all like the winding, paved road circuits of Europe. In Europe racing was done with expensive sports cars or with pure race cars. Here it was done with stock cars, huge American passenger cars modified for racing.

"That," says Mario, "was probably the happiest moment of my life. Instead of looking at racing as something that was way down the road for us, this was something we could begin working on right away!"

They promised each other that they would somehow build one of these stock cars. They had no idea how, but they decided: "Let's stumble through it," Mario recalls. "We were possessed."

Ci sono molte corse in America! Indeed, much racing in America.

It took Mario and Aldo three years of learning the working of American cars, and of raising funds at the rate of $5 apiece from school chums—"investors" in the racing team—to get a race car ready. It was a 1948 Hudson Hornet. As the 1959 season opened at little Nazareth Speedway, a half-mile oval, the twins realized they still had a problem. "One car, two of us," says Aldo. "We decided to flip a coin for who would drive the first race, and we would take turns after that."

Neither twin had ever driven on an oval, let alone on dirt, but the Andretti blood must have risen. "I got to drive first, and I won," says Aldo. "Then Mario won. We won a stretch of about nine or 10 races in a row. It got to be a spectacular for the promoters to start the Andretti boys in the rear and let us charge through the field."

CHRONOLOGY

1492

Cristoforo Colombo (Christopher Columbus), sailing for the Spanish rulers Ferdinand and Isabella, lands on an island in the Western Hemisphere. Over the next dozen years, he makes three more voyages to the New World.

1497

Giovanni Caboto (John Cabot), sailing for the English ruler Henry VII, lands on the North American continent.

1490s

The newly discovered world is labeled "America" by a German cartographer after the Italian explorer and cartographer Amerigo Vespucci.

1657

Fleeing religious persecution in Europe, 150 Italians immigrate to New Amsterdam (later New York). They are from a Protestant sect, the Waldensians.

1681–1711

Italian priest Eusebio Chino (Kino) explores Spanish California territory and establishes missions in what is now Mexico and the southwestern United States.

1773

Italian writer and intellectual Filippo Mazzei arrives in Virginia and forms a friendship with Thomas Jefferson. Mazzei's writings influence Jefferson's political thinking.

1782

William Paca, signer of the Declaration of Independence,

becomes the first Italian American to be elected the governor of a U.S. state, Maryland.

1837

John Phinizy (Finizii) is the first Italian American to serve as mayor of an American city, Augusta, Georgia.

1849

The telephone is invented by Antonio Meucci. This invention is often and falsely credited to Alexander Graham Bell.

1880s

Italian Americans create the wine industry in northern California and establish family wineries under the names Gallo, Rossi, Petri, and others.

1880–1920

Millions of Italians immigrate to America. Most are from southern Italy.

1891

Eleven Italian immigrants are lynched in New Orleans after being found not guilty of the murder of a policeman.

1892

Ellis Island, New York, is opened as an immigrant-processing center. Over the next sixty-two years, millions of Italians pass through Ellis Island, which they refer to as the Island of Tears.

1908

Joseph Carabelli is the first Italian American elected to the U.S. House of Representatives.

1910

Italian immigrants lead a strike in Chicago and form the Amalgamated Clothing Workers of America.

1913

Rudolph Valentino immigrates to America; in the 1920s, he becomes a major film star.

1916

Fiorello La Guardia is elected to the U.S. House of Representatives. In 1933, he is elected mayor of New York City.

1917

A literacy test becomes part of U.S. immigration requirements with the intention of reducing immigration from southern and eastern Europe, including Italy.

1920

Italian immigrant anarchists Nicola Sacco and Bartolomeo Vanzetti are arrested for robbery and murder. After a highly publicized trial and appeal, they are eventually executed in 1927.

1932

Italian American Joe DiMaggio begins his illustrious career as a baseball player.

1939

Pietro di Donato publishes his novel about Italian immigrant life, *Christ in Concrete*.

1942

Thousands of Italian Americans living in California are forced by the government into internment camps or are relocated to new homes in the interior of the state when Italy and the United States become opponents in World War II.

1952

Italian American Rocky Marciano wins the heavyweight boxing championship.

1967

Jim Delligatti invents the "Big Mac" sandwich for his three

McDonald's restaurants in Pittsburgh. Mario Andretti wins his first Daytona 500 championship.

1969

Mario Puzo publishes his novel *The Godfather*.

1971

Lido (Lee) Anthony Iacocca takes over leadership of the Chrysler Corporation and brings the company back from bankruptcy.

1972

Francis Ford Coppola releases the first of his trilogy of films, *The Godfather*.

1982

Mario Cuomo is elected governor of the state of New York.

1984

Legislator Geraldine Ferraro accepts the Democratic Party's nomination for vice president of the United States.

1994

Leon Panetta is appointed White House chief of staff by President Bill Clinton.

2001

Rudolph Giuliani, mayor of New York City, becomes "America's Mayor" as he leads the city in the days following the terrorist attacks of September 11.

2002

Nancy D'Alesandro Pelosi becomes the first woman elected to the position of U.S. House of Representatives minority leader.

2004

Sofia Coppola wins an Oscar for her original screenplay, *Lost in Translation*.

FOR FURTHER RESEARCH

Histories

Richard D. Alba, *Italian Americans: Into the Twilight of Ethnicity.* Englewood Cliffs, NJ: Prentice-Hall, 1985.

Kenny L. Brown, *The Italians in Oklahoma.* Norman: University of Oklahoma Press, 1980.

Pellegrino D'Acierno, ed., *The Italian American Heritage: A Companion to Literature and the Arts.* New York: Garland, 1999.

Richard Dillon, *North Beach: The Italian Heart of San Francisco.* Novato, CA: Presidio, 1985.

Edwin Fenton, *Immigrants and Unions: A Case Study: Italians and American Labor, 1870–1920.* New York: Arno, 1975.

Dorothy and Thomas Hoobler, *The Italian American Family Album.* New York: Oxford University Press, 1994.

Luciano J. Iorizzo and Salvatore Mondello, *The Italian Americans.* Boston: Twayne, 1980.

Salvatore J. LaGumina, *Wop! A Documentary History of Anti-Italian Discrimination in the United States.* Toronto, Canada: Guernica, 1999.

Salvatore J. LaGumina et al., eds., *The Italian American Experience: An Encyclopedia.* New York: Garland, 2000.

Michael La Sorte, *La Merica: Images of Italian Greenhorn Experience.* Philadelphia: Temple University Press, 1985.

Jerre Mangione and Ben Morreale, *La Storia: Five Centuries of the Italian American Experience*. New York: HarperPerennial, 1992.

Julia Volpelletto Nakamura, "The Italian American Contribution to Jazz," *Italian Americana*, vol. 8, no. 1, Fall/Winter 1986.

Humbert S. Nelli, *The Business of Crime: Italians and Syndicate Crime in the United States*. New York: Oxford University Press, 1976.

———, *From Immigrants to Ethnics: The Italian Americans*. Oxford, England: Oxford University Press, 1983.

Andrew F. Rolle, *The Immigrant Upraised: Italian Adventurers and Colonists in an Expanding America*. Norman: University of Oklahoma Press, 1968.

Lydio F. Tomasi, *The Italian in America: The Progressive View, 1891–1914*. New York: Center for Migration Studies, 1972.

Autobiographies, Memoirs, and Oral Histories

A. Kenneth Ciongoli and Jay Parini, eds., *Beyond the Godfather: Italian American Writers on the Real Italian American Experience*. Hanover, NH: University Press of New England, 1997.

David Steven Cohen, ed., *America: The Dream of My Life: Selections from the Federal Writers' Project's New Jersey Ethnic Survey*. New Brunswick, NJ: Rutgers University Press, 1990.

Geraldine Ferraro, *Framing a Life: A Family Memoir*. New York: Scribner, 1998.

Hamilton Holt, ed., *The Life Histories of {Undistinguished} Americans as Told by Themselves*. New York: Routledge, 1990.

Corinne Azen Krause, *Grandmothers, Mothers, and*

Daughters: Oral Histories of Three Generations of Ethnic Women. Boston: Twayne, 1991.

Fiorello H. La Guardia, *The Making of an Insurgent: An Autobiography, 1882–1919.* Philadelphia: J.B. Lippincott, 1948.

Salvatore J. LaGumina, *The Immigrants Speak: Italian Americans Tell Their Story.* New York: Center for Migration Studies, 1979.

Maria Laurino, *Were You Always Italian? Ancestors and Other Icons of Italian America.* New York: W.W. Norton, 2000.

Connie A. Maglione and Carmen Anthony Fiore, *Voices of the Daughters.* Princeton, NJ: Townhouse, 1989.

Joan Morrison and Charlotte Fox Zabusky, *American Mosaic: The Immigrant Experience in the Words of Those Who Lived It.* New York: E.P. Dutton, 1980.

Vincent Panella, *The Other Side: Growing Up Italian in America.* Garden City, NY: Doubleday, 1979.

Mark Rotella, *Stolen Figs and Other Adventures in Calabria.* New York: Northpoint, 2003.

Al Santoli, *New Americans: An Oral History: Immigrants and Refugees in the U.S. Today.* New York: Viking, 1988.

Marianna De Marco Torgovnick, *Crossing Ocean Parkway: Readings by an Italian American Daughter.* Chicago: University of Chicago Press, 1994.

Web Sites

American Italian Defense Association, www.aida-usa.org. AIDA's Web site gives information on "the positive contributions made by Italian Americans" as well as opposing "all forms of discrimination, negative stereotyping, and defamation of Italian Americans."

American Italian Historical Association, www.aiha.fau.edu. The Web site of this organization is for everyone interested in all aspects of the Italians in America: culture, history, literature, folklore, political issues, and more.

National Italian American Foundation, www.niaf.org. This Web site has a wide variety of information on Italian American history and concerns. The organization promotes Italian American education and career advancement, promotes the appointment of Italian Americans to government positions, encourages Italian language and culture instruction, and monitors negative, stereotyped portrayals of Italian Americans in the media and entertainment industries.

Order Sons of Italy, www.osia.org. This organization was established in 1905 as a mutual aid society for Italian immigrants. Today the organization's Web site has information on concerns of interest to Italian Americans, including preservation of Italian American culture and heritage, and closer relations between the United States and Italy. The antidefamation arm of the organization, the Commission for Social Justice, fights racism, prejudice, and stereotyping of all people, not just Italian Americans.

INDEX